D0538720

Aztec Civilization

Don Nardo

LUCENT BOOKS
A part of Gale, Cengage Learning

GALE
CENGAGE Learning™

Detroit • New York • San Francisco • New Haven, Conn • Waterville, Maine • London

GALE
CENGAGE Learning

LIBRARY OF CONGRESS CATALOGING-IN-PUBLICATION DATA

Nardo, Don, 1947-
  Aztec civilization / by Don Nardo.
      p. cm. -- (World history)
  Includes bibliographical references and index.
  ISBN 978-1-4205-0242-8 (hardcover)
  1. Aztecs--Juvenile literature. I. Title.
  F1219.73.N37 2010
  972--dc22
                                                    2009040802

Lucent Books
27500 Drake Rd.
Farmington Hills, MI 48331

ISBN-13: 978-1-4205-0242-8
ISBN-10: 1-4205-0242-5

Printed in the United States of America
1 2 3 4 5 6 7 14 13 12 11 10

Printed by Bang Printing, Brainerd, MN, 1ˢᵗ Ptg., 04/2010

Contents

Foreword

Each year, on the first day of school, nearly every history teacher faces the task of explaining why his or her students should study history. Many reasons have been given. One is that lessons exist in the past from which contemporary society can benefit and learn. Another is that exploration of the past allows us to see the origins of our customs, ideas, and institutions. Concepts such as democracy, ethnic conflict, or even things as trivial as fashion or mores, have historical roots.

Reasons such as these impress few students, however. If anything, these explanations seem remote and dull to young minds. Yet history is anything but dull. And therein lies what is perhaps the most compelling reason for studying history: History is filled with great stories. The classic themes of literature and drama—love and sacrifice, hatred and revenge, injustice and betrayal, adversity and triumph—fill the pages of history books, feeding the imagination as well as any of the great works of fiction do.

The story of the Children's Crusade, for example, is one of the most tragic in history. In 1212 Crusader fever hit Europe. A call went out from the pope that all good Christians should journey to Jerusalem to drive out the hated Muslims and return the city to Christian control. Heeding the call, thousands of children made the journey. Parents bravely allowed many children to go, and entire communities were inspired by the faith of these small Crusaders. Unfortunately, many boarded ships were captained by slave traders, who enthusiastically sold the children into slavery as soon as they arrived at their destination. Thousands died from disease, exposure, and starvation on the long march across Europe to the Mediterranean Sea. Others perished at sea.

Another story, from a modern and more familiar place, offers a soul-wrenching view of personal humiliation but also the ability to rise above it. Hatsuye Egami was one of 110,000 Japanese Americans sent to internment camps during World War II. "Since yesterday we Japanese have ceased to be human beings," he wrote in his diary. "We are numbers. We are no longer Egamis, but the number 23324. A tag with that number is on every trunk, suitcase and bag. Tags, also, on our breasts." Despite such dehumanizing treatment, most internees worked hard to control their bitterness. They created workable communities inside the camps and demonstrated again and again their loyalty as Americans.

These are but two of the many stories from history that can be found in the pages of the Lucent Books World History series. All World History titles rely on sound research and verifiable evidence, and all give students a clear sense of time, place, and chronology through maps and time lines as well as text.

All titles include a wide range of authoritative perspectives that demonstrate the complexity of historical interpretation and sharpen the reader's critical thinking skills. Formally documented quotations and annotated bibliographies enable students to locate and evaluate sources, often instantaneously via the Internet, and serve as valuable tools for further research and debate.

Finally, Lucent's World History titles present rousing good stories, featuring vivid primary source quotations drawn from unique, sometimes obscure sources such as diaries, public records, and contemporary chronicles. In this way, the voices of participants and witnesses as well as important biographers and historians bring the study of history to life. As we are caught up in the lives of others, we are reminded that we too are characters in the ongoing human saga, and we are better prepared for our own roles.

Important Dates at the Time

B.C.
ca. 10,000
Bands of Native Americans migrate into Mexico from the north.

ca. 3500–3300
The world's first cities begin to rise in Mesopotamia (now Iraq).

ca. 1800–300
The first advanced Mesoamerican culture—the Olmecs—thrives.

A.D.
ca. 1000
Viking seafarers become the first Europeans to land in North America.

B.C. ca. 10,000   ca. 3500–3300   ca. 1800–300   A.D. ca. 1000   1325   1415   1428   1453

1325
The Aztecs establish their capital city of Tenochtitlan.

1415
England's king Henry V defeats the French at Agincourt.

1428
The Aztecs establish the Triple Alliance with two neighboring peoples.

1453
The Ottoman Turks capture the Byzantine capital of Constantinople.

of the Aztec Civilization

ca. 1484
Hernán Cortés, the future conqueror of the Aztecs, is born in Spain.

1502
Montezuma II becomes king of the Aztecs.

1517
Religious reformer Martin Luther initiates the Protestant Reformation.

1492
Italian navigator Christopher Columbus stumbles onto the so-called New World.

1511
Spain establishes a thriving colony on the island of Cuba.

ca. 1484   1492   1502   1511   1517   1519   1520   1521   1522   1821

1519
Cortés lands with a small army in Mexico.

1520
The great Italian painter Raphael dies; Cortés has Montezuma executed, igniting a major Aztec uprising.

1521
The Aztec capital of Tenochtitlan falls to Cortés after a long siege.

1522
Members of explorer Ferdinand Magellan's crew return to Spain after sailing around the world.

1821
Mexico gains its independence from Spain.

A Clash of Similar Cultures

In 1519 Spanish soldier and adventurer Hernán Cortés landed with a force of more than five hundred soldiers on Mexico's eastern coast. This marked the first major European foray into Central America. Modern scholars use the term *Mesoamerica* to refer to this part of the world before the Europeans or other outsiders arrived, and they collectively refer to the various Native American peoples who lived there as Mesoamericans.

Chief among these Mesoamerican peoples, Cortés discovered, were the Aztecs. In the course of the preceding century, they had created a large empire. Stretching from Mexico's Atlantic coast westward to the Pacific Ocean, it encompassed some 5 million people, living in more than four hundred towns and cities. The Spanish, who had expected to find the region sparsely inhabited by disorganized primitives, were amazed. In particular, the new-comers were stunned by the size and splendor of the Aztecs' capital city, Tenochtitlan. Built on an island in a huge lake, it covered some 5 square miles (13sq. km) and had at least two hundred thousand residents; at the time, that made it the fourth largest city in the world (after Paris, France; Venice, Italy; and Constantinople, Turkey). It was filled with enormous stone structures, including towering pyramids with temples erected at their summits. One of Cortés's soldiers, Bernal Diaz del Castillo, later wrote:

> When we saw all those cities and villages built in the water, and other great towns on dry land, and that straight and level causeway leading to [Tenochtitlan], we were astounded. These great towns and [huge temple-pyramid] buildings rising from the water, all made of stone, seemed like an enchanted vi-

sion. . . . Indeed, some of our soldiers asked whether it was not all a dream. It is not surprising, therefore, that I should write in this vein. It was all so wonderful that I do not know how to describe this first glimpse of things never heard of, seen, or dreamed of before.[1]

A Destiny to Rule Others

The great size of Tenochtitlan and the overall organization and grandeur of the Aztec Empire underscored a surprising revelation for the Spanish. Namely, this native civilization was in many ways equal to that of Spain and other European nations. True, the Aztecs did not have cannons or guns. But they did have a large, well-trained army equipped with weapons nearly as lethal as European firearms. That made the natives worthy opponents militarily speaking, foes not to be taken lightly.

Moreover, the Spanish observed numerous other similarities between the two civilizations. Each had a hierarchy (ladder) of social classes that featured royalty at the top, followed by nobles and priests, commoners, and then slaves. There were also some striking political parallels. For example, both

A map of ancient Aztec civilization and various sites in Mexico, including Tenochtitlan and Teotihuacan.

the Aztecs and Spanish believed in the divinely inspired destiny and right of one people and empire to rule over others. As anthropologist Norman Bancroft-Hunt puts it:

they [both] came from backgrounds dominated by royal lineages [family lines] and in which the acquisition of power and wealth were important. And they were both religious zealots [fanatics]. Cortés [came from] a tradition that [held] that [as a representative of God and Spain's king] he was destined to establish Spanish sovereignty and Spanish belief in the new lands he came to conquer. [The Aztec ruler], Montezuma, [had] a belief in his own incarnation as the sun deity of

Tenochtitlan, the capital of the Aztec empire, surprised the Spanish with its size and grandeur.

the Aztecs, with an inviolable [sacred] right to rule by reason of his descent from the royal families of the Aztec ancestors.[2]

Thus, both Cortés and Montezuma believed in a world in which the superiority of some peoples over others was an accepted norm and the strong had every right to rule over the weak. These concepts were the driving forces behind the rise of Spain's empire and the no less impressive realm the Aztecs created.

Religious Parallels

The point that the Aztecs and Spanish were "religious zealots" is also well taken. It was not merely that both peoples were religiously devout. Rather, setting aside the fact that the Aztecs worshipped multiple gods and the Christians only one, there were a number of astonishing similarities between the two belief systems. Both had stories about an ancient war in heaven, for example. The Christian version, in which God and the good angels defeat Satan and the bad angels, itself has parallels with tales in older European faiths. The ancient Greeks, for instance, had a myth about the Olympian gods, led by Zeus, vanquishing an earlier race of gods, the Titans. In the Aztec version, no less than four wars involving divine beings take place, each during the climax of a previous historical age.

It is also interesting that the Aztecs believed that giants inhabited Earth during the earliest age. Both the Christian and Greek creation stories include early races of giants as well. Perhaps the most famous reference to them is the one in the Bible. The book of Genesis says, "There were giants in the Earth in those days."[3]

The Aztecs and Spanish shared several other religious beliefs. One involved a great flood that destroyed most of the human race in the distant past. In the Christian version, itself based on flood legends from ancient Mesopotamia, God warns Noah about the coming deluge; Noah and his family then construct a big boat and survive the disaster. In the Aztec version, the water goddess Chalchiuhtlicue warns a man named Coxcox and his wife, Xochiquetzal; they ride out the catastrophe in a hollowed-out log.

No less remarkable is that tales of the bloody sacrifice of divine beings lay at the heart of both faiths. For the Spanish and other Christians, of course, the key event was Jesus Christ's willing crucifixion, meant to ensure salvation for humanity. Similarly, the Aztecs believed that several of their early gods had died by casting themselves into a fire. This was done to make sure the sun would shine and allow life, including humans, to thrive on Earth. "Let this be," the deities supposedly declared as they stood at the fire's edge. "Through us the sun may be revived. Let all of us die!"[4]

Worthy Opponents

Some significant differences existed between the Spanish and Aztec cultures, to

The World Covered by Water

Carleton Beals, a noted scholar of Central America, penned this rendition of the Aztec legend of a great flood that caused the fourth destruction of life on Earth:

Disgusted with mankind, the gods charged [the] Goddess of Water [Chalchiuhtlicue] to punish them. [She] went down to the valley and entered a small house where lived an honorable married couple. . . . The man was named Coxcox and the woman was called Xochiquetzal. [The goddess told them:] "There will come a great flood that will overwhelm the Earth. Cut down this [cypress tree] and get inside it. Take with you the fire from your hearth.". . . Hastening back to the cloud-crowned mountain, she looked sternly in the four cardinal directions, then waved her banner with both hands and all her strength. [Lightning] flashed, thunder crackled [and] rain and hail pounded the Earth and mighty torrents swept over everything—fields, towns, and cities. [But] the privileged couple floated safely in the [tree] trunk [until] the waters finally subsided. The Earth dried out, and [the] couple gave thanks to divine providence. They were blessed with many children, but they were all dumb, till finally a bird taught them various languages.

Carleton Beals, *Stories Told by the Aztecs*. New York: Abelard-Schuman, 1970, pp. 30–31.

be sure. For instance, the Aztecs did not have an all-consuming desire to acquire money and valuables as the Spanish did. And the two peoples had very different sorts of writing, counting, and calendar-making systems. However, these and other dissimilarities ultimately pale in comparison to the similarities.

The Aztecs and Spanish were in many ways worthy opponents. A number of modern depictions of their epic confrontation portray it as the subjugation of a weaker, unsophisticated people by a stronger, more advanced one. But this picture is misleading. In truth, it was more a clash of similar cultures and almost equally forceful adversaries. Furthermore, under somewhat altered circumstances and timing, the outcome of that conflict might have been very different. When Cortés arrived, Aztec civilization was only a couple of centuries old and had not yet begun to explore its full potential. Had it been a few centuries older and more mature, it may have been able to survive the Spanish onslaught. Also, the Aztecs had no practical immunity to some of the terrible diseases the Europeans brought with them. If the natives *had* possessed such immunity, the millions of them who died from these diseases would have lived, again making the continued existence of the Aztec nation more likely.

As it turned out, that nation was swept away. However, many of its inhabitants did survive. And their descendants kept alive many aspects of Aztec culture, some of which are still practiced today. Supplementing this knowledge are a number of archaeological finds and some surviving Spanish accounts of the Aztecs before their fall. Thanks to these combined sources, historians have pieced together a surprisingly vivid picture of the Aztecs, their beliefs, and their everyday lives. This allows modern readers, as one expert phrases it, "to appreciate and admire the achievements of that long-gone, magnificent civilization."[5]

Chapter One

The Rise of the Aztecs

Some of what is known about the Aztecs and their impressive civilization comes from surviving writings by the Aztecs themselves. Still more information about them was gathered by Spanish writers who witnessed the Aztecs' fall or lived in Mexico in the years immediately following that epic event. Several of the latter accounts were penned by priests. One of them, a Dominican friar named Diego Durán, was born in Spain in 1537 and had moved to Mexico, then called New Spain, as a young boy. He learned the Aztecs' language, Nahuatl. He also traveled extensively through the lands of the former Aztec Empire, observed the way the natives lived, and as an adult wrote three books about them. His fascination and respect for them comes through in his heartfelt words. In one of his books, Durán writes:

So great were the feats and exploits of the Aztecs, so full of adventure, that those who are not acquainted with these exploits and with these people will enjoy hearing of their ancient customs and of their origins and descendants.[6]

One item of note that emerges from Durán's books is that he did not call his subjects *Aztecs*. That term was coined some two centuries later by German naturalist Alexander von Humboldt and other European scholars. The name stuck and became the common, accepted term for that native people in modern writings. However, Durán and other Spaniards of his day used the name that the natives called themselves—the Mexica (from which the term *Mexico* clearly derives).

Mesoamerican Predecessors

In his studies, Durán learned that the Mexica were relative latecomers to Mesoamerica (central and southern Mexico), where they built their vast empire. A number of native peoples preceded them, they told him, a fact that modern archaeology has confirmed. Indeed, bands of hunter-gatherers entered what is now Mexico from the north perhaps as early as 10,000 B.C. Evidence shows that crude attempts at agriculture began in the region circa 6000 B.C. and that by roughly 3400 B.C. the first permanent settlements appeared. In about 1800 B.C. or somewhat later, agriculture became more intensive, with maize (corn), beans, and squash emerging as the principal crops. This reliable food supply stimulated population increases. And during the two millennia that followed, a number of villages grew into prosperous urban centers.

The first local natives whose cities and villages became the building blocks of a nation-state were the Olmecs. That state, situated along the northern coast of central Mexico, thrived from about 1800 to 300 B.C. More than just the first major civilization in the region, it was also highly influential, providing a cultural model for later Mesoamerican peoples. California State University scholar Manuel Aguilar-Moreno says:

Although the origins of the Olmecs are unknown at this time, the Olmec

This map shows cities in Aztec, Maya, Zapotec, and Olmec civilizations. The Olmecs' was the first civilization in the area and greatly influenced the other cultures.

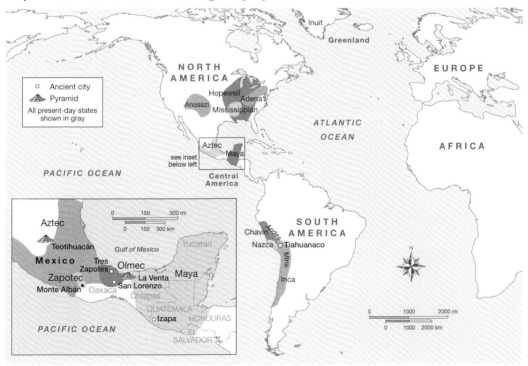

The Teotihuacano civilization's central city was Teotihuacan, shown here.

contributions to Mesoamerican culture are significant, including a style of art that spread throughout Mesoamerica and perhaps the first great religious or ceremonial organization. For these contributions, their culture is referred to as the "Mother Culture of Mesoamerica.". . . Whether this diffusion of influence occurred because of a ruling empire, a common set of religious beliefs, or through a vast trade network or colonization remains unknown.[7]

Some of the Mesoamerican peoples who coexisted with the Olmecs eventually succeeded them as the leading cultures in the region. They included the Zapotecs, whose homeland lay directly south of the Olmec lands, and the Maya, who inhabited the Yucatán Peninsula and the areas south of it. The Zapotecs seem to have invented the complex calendar used by most of the later Mesoamericans, including the Aztecs. The Maya reached their height of prosperity in what scholars call the Classic period of ancient Mesoamerica. It lasted from about A.D. 200 to 900. The Maya excelled at painting and sculpture and erected numerous large cities featuring lofty stone pyramids and religious temples. They are also famous for suddenly abandoning their southern cities in the 700s and 800s; this may have been because of prolonged, severe droughts.

Another Mesoamerican civilization that thrived in the Classic period was located farther north, in the Valley of Mexico (a huge geological basin, ringed by mountain ranges, in central Mexico). Its central city was Teotihuacan, lying northeast of Lake Texcoco. The vast city, covering 12 square miles (31sq. km), was dominated by a central ceremonial area featuring more than a hundred temples, shrines, and altars. Biggest of all was a structure the Aztecs called the Pyramid of the Sun. At 246 feet (75m) in height, it is the third largest pyramid in the world.

The exact origins and identity of the Teotihuacanos remain unknown. But there is no doubt that they exerted a profound cultural influence on later Mesoamerican peoples. After Teotihuacan was burned and abandoned in the eighth century, people from across Mesoamerica, eventually including the Aztecs, made pilgrimages there. "To the Aztecs," noted anthropologist Michael E. Smith writes:

the city was a mystical and sacred place, the birthplace of the gods, and they named the ruins Teotihuacan, which means "city or place of the gods" in Nahuatl. The modern popular names of the main pyramids (sun and moon) and the "Street of the Dead" are translations of the Aztec terms. We do not know what the city or its buildings were called in the Classic period, nor what language(s) were spoken there. A number

of Aztec traits can be traced back to Teotihuacan. The Aztecs were the only other Mesoamerican culture to build a city as large as Teotihuacan, or to create a zone of economic and political influence as extensive as Teotihuacan's.[8]

The Great Migration

Thus, Teotihuacan had long been more or less a ghost town by the time the Aztecs appeared in the Valley of Mexico in the 1200s. The exact location of their original homeland remains uncertain. But there are numerous myths that claim they came from a land called Aztlan, lying far to the north. Some scholars think that Aztlan might have been a real place, perhaps located in northern Mexico or

Aztecs migrating to the Valley of Mexico in the 1200s.

the southern United States. Others suspect that it was only mythical.

Whether or not Aztlan was real, the Aztecs believed that long ago the gods had ordered them and other Nahuatl speakers to leave that place and migrate southward. There were at least seven separate groups, of which the Mexica, or Aztecs, were but one. During the journey, most of the groups went their own ways and settled in various parts of Mexico. As for the Aztecs, they continued southward, stopping periodically to build houses, farms, and temples. Repeatedly, they stayed in one place for ten or twenty years and then moved on.

Always, the people were compelled to keep going by their priests, who claimed to be receiving visions and orders from their fierce patron god, Huitzilopochtli. That deity said that they would eventually see a distinct sign indicating they had reached their ultimate homeland. That sign would consist of a big eagle sitting atop a cactus growing out of a rock. On that spot, Huitzilopochtli said:

> we shall find our rest, our comfort, our grandeur. There our name will be praised and our Aztec nation made great. The might of our arms will be known and the courage of our brave hearts. . . . We shall become lords of gold and silver, of jewels and precious stones. . . . There we will build the city that is to be queen, that is to rule over all others in the country.[9]

Sometime in the 1250s, as roughly calculated by modern scholars, the wandering Aztecs reached the Valley of Mexico. At first, they did not see the sign their god had predicted. And finding all the fertile land occupied by other peoples, they were forced to settle in a desolate region called Chapultepec (meaning "grasshopper hill"). The newcomers were not very welcome. So it did not take long for some of the neighboring peoples to drive them out of Chapultepec. The king of Culhuacan, a region near Lake Texcoco's southern shore, allowed the refugees to settle in a snake-infested swamp near the lakeshore. But as time went on, the Culhua and Aztecs squabbled, and the latter had to flee once more.

It was then, in about the year 1325, while roaming along the lake, that the weary and bedraggled Aztecs finally found their prophesied homeland. According to their official mythology, they suddenly came upon a cactus growing from a large rock:

> And on top of it [was] an eagle with its wings extended toward the rays of the sun, taking its heat in the coolness of the morning. [When] they saw it, [the Aztecs] bowed down in reverence, [while] the eagle, when he saw them, bowed down, lowering his head. . . . When they saw the eagle bow, [they] began to cry. . . . "Who made us worthy of so much grace and greatness and excellence?" [they asked]. "We have attained what we were searching for, and we have found our city and site, thanks to the

This drawing depicts when the Aztecs encountered an eagle on top of a cactus. This signified to them that this was their homeland and they founded Tenochtitlan.

Lord of Creation and to our god Huitzilopochtli."[10]

(Hundreds of years later, the Republic of Mexico chose to commemorate this pivotal moment in the region's history. Today the Mexican flag shows a mighty eagle perched atop a cactus on a rock.)

The City in the Lake

Convinced that they had found both their rightful homeland and their destiny, the Aztecs set about establishing their capital city. They named it Tenochtitlan, meaning "place of the cactus on the rock." At first, it was small and humble. As scholar Brian M. Fagan puts it:

A more unprepossessing [unattractive] location for a future capital city it would be hard to imagine. Initially, Tenochtitlan was little more than a hamlet on a swampy island at the southern end of Lake Texcoco, the lake that once filled much of the Valley of Mexico. But the Aztecs were nothing if not tough and resourceful.[11]

Indeed, the Aztecs once more proved themselves practical, hard working, and able to adapt quickly to new and difficult

Aztecs building a chinampa. *Chinampas were raised gardens in swamps that were an important part of Aztec agriculture.*

Cloudless Skies and Unrelenting Heat

The abandonment of the southern Mayan cities in the 800s remains a subject of debate among scholars. But many of them now think that severe droughts were the primary culprit. Brian Fagan, a leading historian of archaeology, suggests a believable scenario:

Even at the distance of more than a millennium, we can see the demise of Mayan civilization in the southern lowlands [of Central America] playing out like a Greek tragedy. The droughts begin [and] the reservoirs begin to run dry. For generations, the people have considered their [leaders] to be the infallible guardians of the harvests and Mayan life. But now they have feet of clay [because they] are powerless in the face of the mocking, cloudless skies and unrelenting heat. Tikal and Copan and other cities like them fall apart. Social disorder erupts in the wake of persistent hunger and water shortages. The commoners rise in protest against the bloated nobility. They desert their leaders and scatter through the countryside, leaving mere handfuls of [people] squatting among the ruins. An apocalyptic scenario, perhaps, but entirely plausible, given the vulnerability of Mayan civilization to multiyear droughts.

Brian Fagan, *The Great Warming: Climate Change and the Rise and Fall of Civilizations.* New York: Bloomsbury, 2008, pp. 151–52.

circumstances. Their efforts to create a powerful city-state out of almost nothing were successful in large part because they skillfully applied agricultural practices that had long been utilized by Mesoamerican peoples. In particular, they erected an immense and complex system of *chinampas.* These were raised gardens that rested in reclaimed swamps. In his book about Aztec civilization, scholar Warwick Bray explains why the Aztecs were so efficient and productive:

All plants, except maize, spent the early weeks of growth in nursery beds where the seedlings were carefully tended. A layer of mud was spread over part of the chinampa and allowed to harden until it could be cut up into rectangular blocks, then the gardener poked a hole in each block, dropped in a seed, and covered it with manure, [which consisted of] human dung which was collected from the city latrines for sale to the farmers. The seedlings were watered in dry weather and protected against sudden frosts. Then at the appropriate time they were transplanted to the main beds and mulched with vegetation cut from the swamps.[12]

The Aztecs also created large stretches of fertile farmland on the shores near the island-city. The combination of these farms and the chinampas not only transformed the surrounding terrain, but also created enormous, stable food supplies. So it is not surprising that the population of Tenochtitlan and the rest of central Mexico increased by a factor of five during the mid-to-late 1300s. The Aztecs also bent the local geography to their needs by building inventive systems of dikes and canals across the vast lake.

Tenochtitlan's political power grew somewhat more slowly, however. At first, the Aztecs could not stand up to other, more established local peoples. The strongest of these were the Tepanecs, who dwelled on the lake's western shore, and the Acolhua, on the eastern shore. For a while, Aztec leaders recognized the authority of the

Montezuma's Law Code

In one of his books about the Aztecs, Catholic friar Diego Durán lists the laws attributed to the fifteenth-century king Montezuma I. They include several relating to social life and customs, some of which seem overly strict by modern standards:

1. The king must never appear in public except when the occasion is extremely important and unavoidable. . . .
5. The great lords [nobles], who are twelve [in number], may wear special [cotton] mantles of certain make and design, and the minor lords, according to their valor and accomplishments, may wear others. . . .
7. The commoners will not be allowed to wear cotton clothing, under pain of death, but can use only garments [made] of maguey fiber. . . .
8. Only the great noblemen and valiant warriors are given license to build a house with a second story. For disobeying this law, a person receives the death penalty.
9. Only the great lords are to wear labrets [lip plugs], ear plugs, and nose plugs of gold and precious stones. . . .
14. There is to be a rigorous law regarding adulterers. They are to be stoned and thrown into the rivers or to the buzzards.

Diego Durán, *The History of the Indies of New Spain*, trans. Doris Heyden. Norman: University of Oklahoma Press, 1994, pp. 209–10.

Tepanecs and provided them with tribute (taxlike payments acknowledging submission to someone stronger). It appears that these payments often took the form of military service under Tepanec generals.

The Triple Alliance and the Empire

It did not take long for the Aztec soldiers working for Tepanec generals to gain a reputation as skilled, tough warriors. And under a succession of effective Aztec kings—including Huitzilihuitl, Chimalpopoca, and Itzcoatl—that reputation grew, as did Tenochtitlan and the Aztec state. By the 1420s, the Aztecs had become strong enough to challenge their overlords, the Tepanecs. Sometime in 1426 or 1427, the Tepanec king hugely increased demands for tribute from the Aztecs. And King Itzcoatl responded by boldly gathering a coalition of local peoples to resist the Tepanecs. In 1428 the Aztecs joined forces with the Acolhua, the town of Tlacopan (occupied by Tepanecs who opposed their own king), and the Huexotzinco, a people from a neighboring valley. The allies attacked and soundly defeated the Tepanecs.

After this pivotal event in Mesoamerican history, the Huexotzinco returned to their valley. And Tlacopan and the Acolhua joined with the Aztecs in forming the Triple Alliance. Each promised not to make war on the others and to continue to support the alliance's conquests of other peoples. All tribute collected from defeated peoples was to be divided fairly among the three member states. In fact, one scholar has called the new empire lorded over by the alliance a "tribute machine." Regular supplies of valuable commodities, he says:

> were ensured by orchestrated campaigns of taxation, political marriages, and veiled threats of armed force. . . . Tax collectors supervised carefully specified tribute payments to be made at regular intervals [and] by the time of the Spanish conquest, one of Tenochtitlan's palaces alone was sufficiently well provisioned by tribute to house and feed the entire Spanish [army]. Tribute took many [forms, including firewood], gold dust for fine ornaments, tropical bird feathers for ceremonial headdresses and warriors' uniforms, cotton mantles, tree gum, and animal skins.[13]

The empire's expansion continued for many years. Under Itzcoatl and his Acolhuac counterpart, most of the other peoples in the Valley of Mexico came under the sway of the Triple Alliance. After Itzcoatl's death in 1440, he was succeeded by Montezuma I. (Scholars also use Moctezuma, Motecuhzoma, and other spellings.) The new king, who ruled for twenty-eight years, engaged in several new conquests that extended far past the Valley of Mexico's borders. Much, though not all, of Mesoamerica steadily came under the control of the Triple Alliance. Montezuma also replaced a number of local kings with Aztec puppet rulers and began construction of the so-called Great Temple in Tenochtitlan. In addition, he compiled a new law code that strongly favored nobles over members of the lower classes.

Under a later capable Aztec king, Ahuitzotl (reigned 1486–1502), another major turning point occurred. Namely, the Aztecs became the uncontested dominant member of the alliance. From that time on, the alliance and all it controlled was essentially the Aztecs' personal empire in all but name. After Ahuitzotl died, his nephew, Montezuma II, took control of this vast realm. A stern, perhaps even ruthless, ruler, Montezuma used strong-arm tactics to control his nobles and keep his foreign subjects in line.

There was one local people that the new king could neither bully nor defeat, however. The Tlaxcalans, who lived in the valley lying east of Lake Texcoco, had long managed to survive attacks by the Triple Alliance. And they were able to remain free of Montezuma's control as well. At the time, no one realized that Tlaxcala's independence would soon prove a major factor in the Aztecs' demise. For soon the Tlaxcalans would connect with an unexpected ally of their own, one that would prove an irresistible foe. In the eighteenth year of Montezuma's reign (1519), several hundred light-skinned strangers landed on Mexico's eastern coast. These men from a distant land the natives had never heard of—Spain—would, with frightening swiftness, bring the long march of Mesoamerica's splendid indigenous civilization to a crashing end.

Chapter Two

Society and Everyday Life

When the Spanish arrived in Mexico in the sixteenth century, they found the area occupied by people with a highly diverse and complex culture. In some ways, Aztec society and its various members resembled their counterparts in most other cultures throughout history, including the Spanish in the 1500s and many modern societies. The Aztecs maintained close family ties and were religiously devout. They also engaged in commonplace activities, such as farming, making clothes, building houses, trading goods, buying and selling in marketplaces, marriage, schooling, and sports. However, if a person today was able to travel backward in time to the Aztec Empire at its height, he or she would be in for a healthy dose of culture shock. Despite many similarities between Aztec society and modern societies, there are some crucial differences. The Aztecs had a number of so-

cial ideas and customs that people today would view as strange, disturbing, or both.

One of the most basic and central of these differences is the manner in which Aztecs of all walks of life viewed their places and roles in society. They believed that their gods had created a balance, or healthy set of conditions, in both the natural world and human society. And it was essential that people maintain that balance at all costs. It was thought that failure to do so would result in the release of harmful supernatural forces, including the wrath of the gods.

The Aztecs maintained this all-important balance in human society mainly by conformity. That is, each social group was seen to have a proper place in the grand scheme of things. And members of all groups were expected to conform to their traditional roles. In the Aztec view, as one modern expert explains:

Society and the entire cosmos [universe] work best when *everything and everyone finds their correct place and conforms to the requirements of that place in the universe*. In this view of the world, it is morally good to fit into your place, to find and stay within the boundaries of your social group and your working profession, and to contribute to the overall balance of society, [so that] doing the right thing means being in the right social place.[14]

Thus, social dissent, nonconformity, and independent thought were almost unheard of in the Aztec world.

The Social Pyramid

It was easy for members of Aztec society to know their "right social place" because the rules of the social classes were drilled into people beginning in early childhood. According to these rules, the top of the social pyramid was occupied by the king, the *tlatoani*, which means "chief speaker" in Nahuatl. He was elected by a select group of nobles and his position was not necessarily hereditary. (In other words, his son or another relative might or might not succeed him on the throne.) In addition to governing the empire, the tlatoani was expected, whenever possible, to expand it in the name of the god Huitzilopochtli.

A group of Aztec nobles. Nobles were called the pipiltin *and thought to be ordained by the gods.*

Directly under the king in social and political rank was the prime minister, or *cihuacoatl*. He carried out most of the day-to-day business of the government and oversaw the empire's financial matters. He also moved into the royal palace and governed Tenochtitlan when the king was away on military campaigns. The cihuacoatl was also one of a handful of highly placed nobles—the *tetecuhtin*—who had distinguished themselves by their valor in battle or in some other way. The nobles in general were called the *pipiltin*. Supposedly they were ordained by the gods to make up a ruling class with special privileges. Among these were the rights to own their own land, to be exempt from paying tribute to the king and from doing menial work, and to have more than one wife.

Nearly everyone else in Aztec society belonged to a lower social class—the *macehualtin*, or "commoners." It was thought that the gods wanted the macehualtin to obey the nobles and to do the diverse jobs that kept society functioning on a regular basis. This group itself had various levels of social status. Highest among the macehualtin were *pochteca*, or traders. They often accumulated a great deal of money and luxuries. Also, because they frequently traveled to foreign lands and towns, they were of great service to the government as spies. After collecting intelligence (information about potential foes), they reported back to government officials in Tenochtitlan. Sixteenth-century Spanish chronicler Bernadino de Sahagun wrote:

When the tradesmen entered [the foreign town of] Tzinactlan, it was still not conquered. When they entered, it was not apparent that they were Mexicans [i.e., Aztecs] because they were disguised and looked like the locals. They wore their hair like the inhabitants of Tzinactlan [and] they tried to imitate them in every way and they learned their language. So they entered incognito [in secret], such that absolutely no one realized they were Mexicans.[15]

Directly beneath the traders on the social ladder were ordinary laborers. In their ranks were farmers, fishermen, weavers, carpenters, stonecutters, shopkeepers, metalworkers, potters, sculptors, and so forth.

Like most macehualtin, they were required to pay tribute to the government on a regular basis. These payments took several forms. Depending on the occupation or situation, they could consist of foodstuffs, cloth, or a set amount of labor, such as working on a government-sponsored construction project, like building a canal. A person could also satisfy his tribute-paying obligation by serving as a soldier for a certain length of time. (There was no standing army; the government raised whatever troops it needed by drafting citizens into temporary military service.)

Lowest among the macehualtin in the social pyramid were serflike individuals called *mayeque*. Though free, they were poor farm laborers who were highly dependent on the rich lords they worked for. In contrast, slaves, or *tla-cotin*, who ranked even lower than the macehualtin, were not free. The slaves included war captives, criminals who lost their freedom as a punishment, or freemen who sold themselves into temporary slavery to pay off a debt. Anthropologist Michael E. Smith says, "Failure to pay tribute was another way to become a slave, with the purchase price going to cover the tribute debt."[16] Slavery among the Aztecs was not hereditary, however; that is, the children of a slave were born free.

Families and Their Houses

Whatever social class one belonged to, in Aztec culture the family was always society's primary unit. Families had both collective and individual dimensions and dynamics. Collectively speaking, people strongly identified themselves with groups of families known as *calpulli* (or *calpolli*). Each consisted of a sort of neighborhood or local ward. Small calpulli had about ten to twenty families, while large ones could have several hundred. The typical calpulli had a small temple where members of the group worshipped. It was run by a priest who was fairly equivalent to a modern parish priest. Administering each calpulli was an elected official called a *calpullec*. His duties included keeping track of who belonged to the group, which families occupied which plots of land, and making sure that each family paid its share of tribute to the government. Members of the calpulli tended his land so that he had time to perform his official duties.

On an individual level, each Aztec family was a close-knit unit. Many (though certainly not all) families appear to have been extended, with grandparents, aunts, and uncles living together with a father, mother, and children. The father was the head of the household and made all financial decisions. His wife took care of the home and raised the children. However, in Aztec society child rearing was also viewed as a collective responsibility. The entire extended family was expected to help look after the young, and any family member who shirked this duty was seen as a lazy, bad person.

Just as society was divided into two main social groups—nobles and commoners—the houses in which families dwelled were of two main kinds. Commoners' houses were usually small, with one or two rooms. Such a house was most often L shaped, had one story, and was constructed of sun-dried clay bricks. A small hearth made of rocks rested in the center of the main room. The sparse furniture included some woven reed mats covering the floor, other mats to sleep on, a few wooden chests to store clothes and other belongings, and sometimes a few low chairs made of reeds. Most houses had a small separate hut in the yard that served as a kitchen.

In contrast, nobles' houses were large and spacious. Usually they were located close to the marketplaces, a privilege that came with high social status. It was common for a well-to-do home to be erected atop a stone platform from 10 to 40 feet (3m to 12m) high and to have two stories.

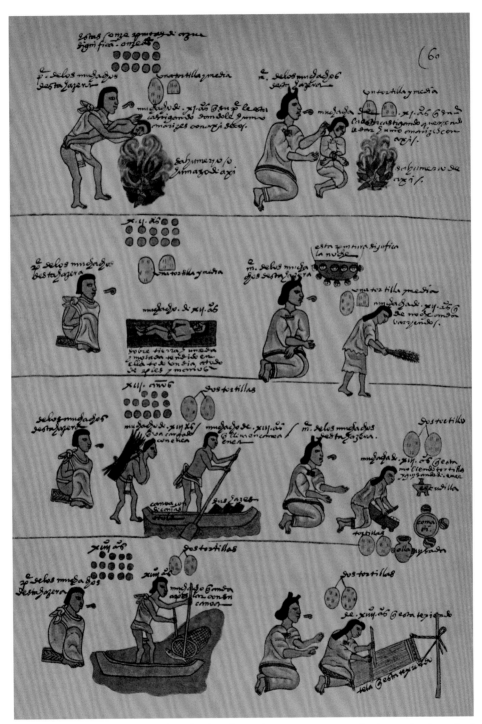

Scenes from daily Aztec life. The family unit was an extremely important part of Aztec culture and worked together every day.

The house's walls were made of brick or stone and covered in stucco (plaster). Surrounding a central courtyard open to the sun were several rooms, including a foyer, kitchen, dining room, one or more sleeping rooms, a meeting room, and some servants' quarters. There were also well-kept gardens, bathing pools, and, in the case of the king, zoos of various kinds. One of the Spanish chroniclers who visited Tenochtitlan before it was destroyed observed an aviary (bird habitat) in the palace of King Montezuma I. He writes:

There was every [type of bird] from the Royal eagle and other smaller eagles, and many other birds of great size, down to tiny birds of many-colored plumage which they use in their green feather work and there are other birds which have feathers of five colors. . . . In this house that I have spoken of there is a great tank of fresh water and in it there are other sorts of birds with long stilted legs, with body, wings, and tail all red.[17]

Women's Status and Duties

Whether a family's lifestyle was humble or lavish, women's roles, duties, and customs were by and large the same. Women were valued and well treated in Aztec society, as partially evidenced by a common adage that describes a bad husband as a man who

A Snapshot of Aztec Women

A sixteenth-century Spanish friar named Bernadino de Sahagun penned this description of some Aztec priestesses in action, which provides a rare snapshot of that society's women:

They were indeed carefully dressed. All good were their skirts, their shifts which they had put on. Some of their skirts had designs of hearts. Some had a mat design like birds' gizzards. Some were ornamented like coverlets [quilts]. Some had designs like spirals or leaves. . . . All had borders, all had fringes, all the women had fringed skirts. And some of their shifts had tawny [yellow-brown] streamers hanging. [And] when they danced, they unbound their hair. Their hair just covered each one of them like a garment. But they brought braids of their hair across their foreheads.

Bernadino de Sahagun, *Florentine Codex: General History of the Things of New Spain*, vol. 1, trans. J.O. Anderson and Charles E. Dibble. Santa Fe, NM: School of American Research and University of Utah, 1950, p. 82.

Women's duties, including making clothes and jewelry such as this Aztec pin, were crucial to Aztec society.

beat or verbally abused his wife. Although a woman's political and social status was less than a man's, women's duties were viewed as crucial to the community, so they were respected. A woman "was vital to the economic condition of her family," explains Manuel Aguilar-Moreno, a California State University scholar. According to Aguilar-Moreno:

A wife owned her own property [clothes, jewelry, and so forth]. She wove materials to be sold at the market as well as to pay tribute to the government. She tended to the family's domestic animals, making sure [they] could be sold at fair prices. [Also] attending to the needs of her community, she prepared meals for offerings at the temple that ultimately fed the priests, as well as meals for warriors as they fought in battle. . . . In giving birth, a woman achieved the recognition and respect of a warrior [and] a woman who died in childbirth was revered as a woman warrior.[18]

In addition to these duties and distinctions, women acted as society's chief matchmakers by negotiating the terms of arranged marriages. They were also midwives who supervised the delivery of babies. And a number of women served as priestesses in the temples of certain gods.

As in all cultures, one of the high moments in an Aztec woman's life was her wedding day. Almost all women married in their teens, sometimes even as young as ten or twelve. (Men generally married in the late teens or early twenties.) The parents and matchmaker first consulted a priest or fortune-teller to make sure the wedding did not take place on an unlucky day.

The ceremony itself began with a big feast at the bride's house. At sunset, she bathed and donned a special wedding outfit, then received a lecture from the family elders, who told her:

> Forever now leave childishness, girlishness [behind]. No longer are you to be like a child. . . . Be most considerate of [people]. Regard [people] with respect, speak well, [and] greet [people] well. By night look [around], take care of the sweeping [and] the laying of the fire. Arise in the deep of night [to start your daily duties].[19]

Following this standard speech, people carried the bride to the groom's house in a procession lit by torches. After four days had passed, there was another feast and an exchange of gifts.

Children and Education

One consequence of a girl marrying before reaching her teens was that she missed out on some of her education. It was customary for all Aztec children, boys and girls alike and both commoners and nobles, to attend a formal school sometime between the ages of ten and twenty. Long before that, however, they received more rudimentary forms of education. At age four, for instance, each child underwent a "growth ritual." His or her ears were pierced and fitted with earrings and the child's limbs, neck, fingers, and nose were vigorously pulled in hopes of promoting proper growth. At the same time, mothers taught girls the basics of weaving and fathers taught boys how to carry water and to do other chores. At age five, the children learned how to perform other duties; at age six still others; and so forth.

Over time, but especially between ages ten and fourteen, parents and other family members applied punishments designed to discourage disobedience, rudeness, laziness, and other unwanted behaviors. The two worst offenses a young person could commit in Aztec society were to engage in sex before marriage and to get drunk. The punishments for these and other sorts of misbehavior were often severe, even abusive by modern standards. The *Codex Mendoza*, written by an unknown Spaniard circa 1540, gives the following examples:

> An eight-year-old boy is being warned by his father not to be deceitful, or he will be punished by being pierced in the body by maguey spikes [big, sharp thorns found on the leaves of the maguey plant]. Likewise they punished them [ten year olds] for being rebellious, beating them with sticks and offering other threats. . . . They punished the eleven-year-old boy or girl who disregarded verbal correction by mak-

ing them inhale chili smoke, which was a serious and even cruel torment.[20]

By the time they were subject to such punishments, most children were already attending formal schools. There were two kinds, the first called a *telpochcalli*, or "youth house," catering to commoners. One could be found in every town, as well as in every neighborhood in Tenochtitlan. There was separate instruction for boys and girls. Boys learned to work on large-scale construction projects and received military training, while girls learned about household duties. Both boys and girls studied Aztec myths and history, along with singing, dancing, and playing instruments. (The latter skills were required for taking part in many religious ceremonies.) The other kind of school was a *calmecac*, or "temple school," for nobles and extremely exceptional commoners. This institution provided training for future governmental leaders, priests, and military officers.

The Public Markets

For Aztecs of both genders, all educational backgrounds, and all ages and professions, one of the most important and popular locations in one's town or city was the public marketplace, or *tianquiztli*. In fact, there was a market in every Aztec community. And the ones

The Great Marketplace

Bernal Diaz del Castillo, a soldier in Cortés's army, penned this vivid description of the great open-air marketplace in Tlatelolco, a town adjoining Tenochtitlan:

Let us begin with the dealers in gold, silver, and precious stones, feathers, cloaks, and embroidered goods, and male and female slaves who are also sold there. . . . Next there were those who sold coarser cloth, and cotton goods and fabrics made of twisted thread, and there were chocolate merchants with their chocolate. In this way you could see every kind of merchandise to be found anywhere in New Spain. . . . There were those who sold sisal cloth and ropes and sandals they wore on their feet, which are made from the same plant. All three were kept in one part of the market, in the place assigned to them, and in another part were the skins of tigers and lions, otters, jackals, and deer, badgers, mountain cats and other wild animals, some tanned and some untanned, and other classes of merchandise.

Bernal Diaz del Castillo, *The Conquest of New Spain*, trans. J.M. Cohen. New York: Penguin, 1963, p. 232.

An Aztec marketplace, called a tianquiztli. *The public marketplace was one of the most popular locations in Aztec cities.*

in the large cities were enormous. The largest market in all the Americas was in Tlatelolco, the bustling city adjoining Tenochtitlan. The Spanish were absolutely astounded by its size and diversity, as revealed in a description of it by none other than Hernán Cortés him-

self, who writes:

[It has] arcades [walkways lined with vendors and commercial stalls] all around, where more than 60,000 people come [to] buy and sell, and where every kind of mer-

Aztec Games

Both children and adults played games in Aztec society. Among the most popular was *patolli*, a large board game utilizing a cross-shaped board with fifty-two squares. The players threw beans like modern players throw dice. And they wagered valuables, such as necklaces, feathers, golden ear plugs, slaves, and even houses, on who would be the first to make it all the way around the board.

The most popular game by far, however, was *ullamaliztli*, the Aztec version of a ball game popular throughout ancient Mesoamerica.

On a large, walled ball court, two teams of players fought to control the *ulli*, a hard rubber ball weighing about 9 pounds (4kg). Using mainly their hips and legs, the members of each team attempted to move the ball down the court and into a stone ring (not unlike a basketball hoop) protruding from a wall. The players wore protective gear made of layers of deerskin, including hip, thigh, and cheek guards and gloves.

An Aztec goal ring used in the game ullamaliztli.

Early Spanish eyewitnesses described the players as phenomenally well conditioned and skilled and the game as exciting but also very rough. Injuries were common and some players even died when the fast-moving ball struck them in an unguarded portion of the face or stomach.

chandise produced in these lands is found. [Included are] ornaments of gold and silver, lead, brass, copper, tin, stones, shells, bones, and feathers. They also sell lime, hewn and unhewn stone, adobe bricks, tiles, and cut and uncut woods of various kinds. There is a street where they sell game and birds of every species found in this land.[21]

To this list could be added all manner of food and drink; cotton thread, cloth, and clothes; paint of every hue; jewelry, pottery, and other craft goods; and much more. People could also go to the market for a haircut or to hire singers, carpenters, and even prostitutes.

Another factor that distinguished the Aztec markets was that they were mostly independent of government control. The markets of earlier Mesoamerican cultures had been largely government run. In contrast, the Aztecs had a free-market system similar to that of the United States and other modern capitalist countries (although the Aztec government did impose certain general market regulations). The Aztecs did not have money in the modern sense. So shoppers and sellers exchanged goods of roughly equal value (the barter system). Prices were based on comparisons with the worth of certain products of standard value, including cacao beans, cotton cloth, and pieces of copper.

The market system was so well organized, vibrant, and practical that it survived the Aztecs' fall from the historical stage. Marketplaces amazingly similar to the ones Cortés saw in the 1500s still exist today across Mexico. This fact is a testimony to the potent legacy of the Aztec people.

Chapter Three

Myths and Religious Beliefs

The importance of religion in Aztec society cannot be overstated. Worship of, and especially sacrifice (offerings) to, the gods, or *teteo*, were fundamental aspects of daily life. The Aztecs felt that there was a very strong connection between people and the natural world around them. And because the gods had constructed that world for various purposes, it was thought that people must devote much of their energies to maintaining that connection. Noted scholar of ancient Mesoamerica, Richard F. Townsend, elaborates:

> Since remote time, the rhythms of life in highland Mexico had been deeply imbedded in the land and the changing seasons [and] to the Aztecs, this interaction of humankind with nature was of profound significance. [It] was affirmed through a calendar of cyclic festivals performed at a network of sacred places in cities and throughout the natural landscape. The religious status and functions of rulers were critical to these relationships, for the Aztec [kings] and their [priests] were obliged to ensure, by means of traditional rituals, the regularity of the seasons, the productivity of the land, and the fertility of crops and animals.[22]

Also because of the divine relationship between the gods and nature, the Aztecs held that certain aspects of the landscape were sacred. These included the sun, mountains, caves, the wind, and water, especially rain, lakes, and rivers. The way that such beliefs translated into worship and daily life is illustrated by the construction of the Aztec capital, Tenochtitlan, in the midst of Lake Texcoco. That location was chosen not simply because it was picturesque,

Templo Mayor, shown at the left, was the central pyramid in the Aztec city of Tenochtitlan in Mexico.

but more so because it honored the gods and one of the holiest aspects of nature—a great lake. Such reverence for nature translated in a similar manner into architecture and city planning. The Aztecs (and other Mesoamerican peoples) often erected temples atop stone pyramids, which were meant to symbolize sacred mountains.

Aztec Creation Stories

The relationships among the gods, the wonders of nature, and the human race were explicitly spelled out in a large collection of colorful Aztec creation myths. The seminal story involves the creator god, Ometeotl. The god of fire and light as well as creation, he was supposedly all knowing and had a dual personality that featured both male and female traits. An old Aztec song about Ometeotl says:

He is the Lord and Lady of Duality. He is Lord and Lady of our maintenance. He is mother and father of the gods, the old god. He is at the same time the god of fire [and] the mirror of day and night. He is the star which illumines all things [and] he is our mother, our father.[23]

Because Ometeotl was both male and female, these opposing aspects of his being came together, mated, and produced four divine sons. Among them were the gods Quetzalcoatl and Huitzilopochtli, who proceeded to create other gods, the world, and humanity. The Aztecs called the world these deities constructed Cemanahuac, meaning "land surrounded by water." This acknowledged the reality that the Aztec homeland and empire were bounded in the east and west by vast oceans. Cemanahuac consisted of a huge horizontal disk with an enormous vertical shaft running through its middle. It was thought that the waters surrounding the disk extended far into the distance and then rose up into wall-like mounds that held up the sky. The disk itself was divided into four quarters, each corresponding to one of the four cardinal directions (east, west, north, and south). But there was also a fifth section in the center—the *axis mundi*, or "world's navel." Meanwhile, beneath the great disk was the underworld, where many people's souls went after they died.

Another important outcome of the emergence of Ometeotl's four sons and the other gods was that some of them fought among themselves. And this ensured a long cosmic struggle, a sort of war in heaven. In their myths, the Aztecs viewed it as a fight between the forces of light and darkness, and of good and evil.[24] This ongoing hostility brought about five successive historical ages, or "suns," the first four of which ended in catastrophe. At the close of the first age, giant jaguars devoured the sun and Earth; the second age ended with the destruction of the world by huge hurricanes; a rain of fire consumed Earth at the end of the third age; and the fourth age concluded with a great flood.

Then came the fifth and present age. (The Aztecs believed that it is destined to end badly, too; supposedly, massive earthquakes will rock the world and

An Aztec sculpture showing the birth of the god Quetzalcoatl.

humans will be eaten by sky monsters.) As the fifth age began, the world was dark and lifeless. Concerned, the gods gathered at Teotihuacan with the goal of making the sun appear and move across the sky each day. After thinking long and hard about what to do, two of the gods, Tecuciztecatl and Nanahuatzin, offered to sacrifice themselves. By leaping into a fire, they said, they would cause the sun to be born. This worked, but the sun refused to move across the sky. So the remaining gods willingly sacrificed themselves, a cataclysmic event that forced the sun to move and thereby made life on Earth possible.

Among the living things that subsequently appeared on Earth were humans. Quetzalcoatl gathered the bones of beings who had died in previous ages and poured blood from the genitals of male gods over these relics. From this mixture sprang the first two people—a man, Cipactonal, and a woman, Oxomoco. Various gods gave them skills, including planting, flower growing, and weaving, and as time went on humans multiplied and prospered.

The Divine Pantheon

The gods whom the Aztecs believed had both created them and continued to watch over them numbered well over a hundred. Some had originated with the small group of Mexica that had migrated into central Mexico centuries before. Others were the deities of other Mesoamerican peoples the Aztecs had conquered; the custom was to in-

A sculpture of Coatlicue, the Aztec goddess known as the "Mother of Gods."

corporate these lesser gods into the Aztec pantheon (group of gods) to help pacify those defeated peoples.

Eventually, the Aztecs had a great many gods, which technically made them polytheists. Yet their unique religion also had certain monotheistic overtones. They saw the creator god Ometeotl as a supreme, all-powerful, and eternal deity not unlike the one worshipped by Jews, Christians, and Muslims. And they might have followed him exclusively if it had not been for an irksome aspect of his character. They believed that he dwelled far away from the world and had little or no interest in humanity. So, to fill this emotional void, they came to recognize many other lesser gods who cared about people and had down-to-earth, humanlike feelings, like passion, pride, and anger. The gods (except for Ometeotl) could also die like humans, as happened when Tecuciztecatl, Nanahuatzin, and other gods sacrificed themselves at Teotihuacan. (Unlike humans, however, the gods could, and often did, return to life.)

The Aztecs also held that the gods inhabited all parts of nature and had mostly indirect and subtle ways of interacting with people. It was thought

A Hymn to the Creator

The Aztecs had songs for many of their gods, much as modern Christians have hymns praising God. This song about Ometeotl, the Aztec creator god, reflects his double personality, containing both male and female traits:

He is the Lord and Lady of Duality
He is the Lord and Lady of our maintenance
He is mother and father of the gods, the old god
He is at the same time the god of fire, who dwells in the navel of fire
He is the mirror of day and night
He is the star which illumines all things, and he is the Lady of the
    shining skirt of stars
He is our mother, our father
Above all, he is Ometeotl who dwells in the place of duality, Omeyocan.

Quoted in Miguel Leon-Portilla, *Aztec Thought and Culture*. Norman: University of Oklahoma Press, 1963, p. 90.

that they visited humans in dreams, for example. The gods could also appear in waking visions or approach people disguised as animals. Most of the time, the gods were benevolent and helped people; but they could also become annoyed with humans and punish them. The chief way to ensure that people stayed on the gods' good side was to worship them on a regular basis.

Although these deities below the supreme Ometeotl were numerous, only a handful was seen as more powerful and/or more important than the others. Among the most respected and feared was Tezcatlipoca, popularly known as the "Lord of the Smoking Mirror." One of Ometeotl's sons, Tezcatlipoca aided his father in various acts of creation, possessed potent magical powers, and had the ability to be everywhere at once. He also severely punished wrongdoers. A prayer to this awe-inspiring god reads,

> O master, O our lord. . . . O night O wind. You see [and] know the things within the trees, the rocks. And behold now, it is true that you know of things within us. You hear us from within, what we say, what we think, our minds, our hearts. It is as if smoke [and] mist arose before you.[25]

The major gods also included a number of fertility deities who ensured that plants, animals, and humans would continue to grow and reproduce. Among these major gods was Tlaloc, the bringer of rain and one of the chief Aztec gods. Other important fertility deities included the earth-mother goddesses Coatlicue and Tonantzin and the goddess of sexual desire, Xochiquetzal. Still another fertility god was the most versatile of the Aztec gods—Quetzalcoatl, the "Feathered Serpent." He was also a creator god, a wind god, the god of learning, and the patron deity of priests. Among the other leading gods were Mictlantecuhtli, chief deity of death and the underworld, and Huitzilopochtli, a god of war and the sun and the beloved patron god (personal protector) of the Mexica/Aztecs.

Temples and Sacrifice

Worship of these gods was both private and public. Private ceremonies took place mostly at small shrines in people's homes. Public worship occurred at community shrines and temples attended by large numbers of people. In cities such as Tenochtitlan, the biggest and most important of these buildings were situated in huge, centrally located ceremonial plazas, or sacred precincts. As one noted scholar puts it, their special religious architecture and rituals constituted "the religious point of authority from which priests and [rulers] communicated with gods and directed the lives of the people who lived below them within the social pyramid."[26] The grand sacred precinct at Tenochtitlan measured 600 feet (183m) by 528 feet (161m) and contained numerous pyramids, shrines, stone walkways, and wide-open gathering places.

The largest structure on the site was the Great Temple, which the Aztecs

An Aztec priest offers up a human sacrifice to the gods.

called the Huey Teocalli. The Spanish called it the Templo Mayor. (Today, scholars most often use the Spanish term.) It consisted of an enormous four-sided pyramid with two shrines sitting side by side at the top; one, painted red, honored Huitzilopochtli, and the other, painted blue, was dedicated to Tlaloc. Those who built the temple believed it occupied the center of the universe. It was also designed to depict that universe in miniature. Scholar Brian M. Fagan writes:

The platform that supported the whole structure of the temple corresponded to the terrestrial [earthly] level of existence. The four tapering tiers of the pyramid itself rose to the summit and represented the celestial [heavenly] levels. . . . The [symbolic] Underworld lay [in chambers] beneath the platform.[27]

Not surprisingly, priests both maintained the Templo Mayor and other shrines and conducted the public ceremonies. Male priests were called *tlamacazqui*; female priests, who were far less common, were known as *cihuatlamacazqui*. Most Aztec priests began their training as children by attending a *calmecac* and learning about the basic religious concepts and rituals. Their duties as full-fledged priests included keeping the sacred fires burning, playing musical instruments at ceremonies, and making sacrifices to the gods. Among the sacrificial offerings were food, smoke from burning incense, and the priests' own blood (obtained by cutting themselves on a regular basis). "Priests must have presented a terrible picture to outsiders," says anthropologist Michael E. Smith. "Their faces and bodies were dyed black. Much of their body was scarred and mutilated from constant bloodletting. Their unwashed hair, worn long, became matted with dried blood."[28]

The most sacred offering to the gods in the Aztec ceremonies was a human life. Special priests known as *tlenamacac* ("fire sellers") performed the killing of the victims, which consisted of cutting out their hearts with flint knives. Spaniard Bernal Díaz del Castillo witnessed this gruesome ceremony and later wrote:

With some knives they sawed open their chests and drew out their palpitating [beating] hearts and offered them to the idols that were there, and they kicked the bodies down the steps [of the pyramid], and the Indian[s] who were waiting below cut off the arms and feet and flayed [sliced] the skin off the faces.[29]

Most of the Spanish, as well as many later outside observers, saw this practice as barbaric, and as a result labeled the Aztecs a primitive people. But that view revealed a fundamental lack of understanding of the Aztec religion. As bloody and harsh as these religious killings were, they were an expression of the Aztecs' heartfelt beliefs about the gods and the creation. They accepted without question that the gods had once willingly given their lives to ensure the world's survival. Therefore, humans owed the gods a huge debt. And the only way that debt could be repaid was in kind—in other words, through shedding human blood on a scale that matched that of the gods' own self-sacrifice. Moreover, the Aztecs believed that if this debt was not paid on a regular basis, the world would be destroyed. This was why blood from still-beating hearts was seen as the most valuable substance that people could offer the gods.

Burial Customs

Other Aztec religious beliefs and customs were connected with funerals, burial, and the afterlife. Friar Diego

The Great Temple Resurrected

February 21, 1978, is one of the most important and exciting days in both Mexican and world archaeology. That day some electrical workers were digging near Mexico City's National Cathedral when they came upon a circular stone some 11 feet (3.4m) across covered with strange carvings. Archaeologists hurried to the site. Recognizing the carvings as Aztec glyphs, they began excavating the area around the stone. Within days, to their astonishment and elation, it became clear that they had found the remains of the Aztecs' great temple, which the Spanish called the Templo Mayor. Excavations continued for the next fifteen years under the direction of Mexico's leading archaeologist, Eduardo M. Moctezuma. In all, more than eight thousand ritual objects were found. Also, diggers unearthed five separate earlier versions of the temple, one overlaying another. (The upper and final version of the building was gone, having been destroyed by the Spanish.) In the years that followed, some of the finds were displayed in museums around the world. The exhibit at the Denver Museum of Nature & Science in Denver, Colorado, alone drew more than 800,000 visitors in the 1992–1993 season.

Durán described funerals and burial in one of his books about the Aztecs. He writes:

> Some people were buried in the fields. Others, in the courtyards of their own homes. Others were taken to shrines in the woods. Others were cremated and their ashes buried in the temples. . . . Dirges [sad songs] similar to our [own] were chanted, and [the dead] were mourned [by conducting] great ceremonies in their honor. At these funerals, [people] ate and drank. . . . [The dead man] was laid out in a room for four days until [all the mourners] had arrived. Gifts were brought to the dead man. And if the deceased was a king or chieftain of a town, slaves were killed in his honor to serve him in the afterlife.[30]

Actually, there was no single afterlife in the Aztec belief system. The soul of a dead person was thought to go to one of several different locations, depending on how he or she had died. Soldiers, sacrificial victims, and women who died in childbirth went to a place of great honor; they joined the sun on its daily journey through the sky. People who died by drowning went to Tlalocan, an earthly paradise overseen by the god Tlaloc. Most others, no matter what social class they belonged to, went to

The Heart and Divine Fire

For the Aztecs, human sacrifice was not only a way to pay back the gods for their own earlier sacrifices. It was also part of a larger, more profound way of looking at the world and the roles the gods and humans had in maintaining its stability, as explained here by scholar Norman Bancroft-Hunt:

Every element in the Aztec world [was] a constant reminder of the role the deities had to play in maintaining order and of the indivisible links between the celestial, middle, and lower realms. . . . All these principals were also evident at an even more personal level, since the human body itself was conceived as a representation of the cosmos, with the head, heart, and liver corresponding to the three divisions. Of these, the heart was animated by a force called *teyolia*, or divine fire, a presence that also existed in sacred mountains, temples, and so forth. Human sacrifice is perhaps more readily understood in this context. Just as the sacred fires burning in temples or the rituals dedicated to the gods "gave life" and animated the world, so the human heart "gave life" to the body. Through sacrifice and the offering of a heart, life was in effect being given back to the gods.

Norman Bancroft-Hunt, *Gods and Myths of the Aztecs*. New York: Smithmark, 1996, p. 100.

Mictlan, the underworld, a dreary abode of eternal darkness.

The Aztecs believed that after four years in Mictlan, a soul forgot all about his or her life on Earth. For this reason, most Aztecs had a sense of foreboding about death and viewed the afterlife as a place of hopelessness and loss of identity. Following the Spanish conquest, European missionaries exploited these negative feelings about life after death with considerable success. The hopeful aspects of the Christian afterlife were highly appealing to many Aztecs and helped to persuade them to adopt the Christian faith.

Chapter Four

Art, Literature, and Learning

The Aztecs possessed a rich culture. It included decorative arts, such as architecture, sculpture, and painting, as well as writing and literature. They also delved into a wide range of learning that included studies of math and astronomy and the creation of complex calendars. These accomplishments were often ignored by the Spanish and other Europeans, who chose instead to point out and condemn the natives' violent side. A modern expert explains:

Today, the cultural achievements of the Aztecs remain obscured by a historical fascination with the human sacrifices and warlike behavior that characterized the Aztec society observed by Cortés [and his soldiers]. Perhaps not surprisingly, these rituals shocked the Spanish and have, until recently, dominated the attention of subsequent genera-

tions of Mesoamerican scholars. [Often] unappreciated are the pictorial writings, poetry, and myths, along with the ceramics [pottery], sculpture, and architecture that seem all the more impressive in the apparent absence of metal tools.[31]

Another reason why the European conquerors didn't appreciate Aztec art and literature was that it was visually and conceptually different than their own art. Aztec architecture, painting, sculpture, poetry, and other arts are extremely heavy with religious symbolism, which was meant to appeal more to the gods than to people. Native sculptures, such as statues and architectural decorations, are a good example. They were usually rendered with a unique mix of exaggerated or abstract features and small, realistic details. This was in a sense a special visual language aimed at divine eyes. Similarly, the bottoms or backs of statues and other sculptures were carefully carved, again with great attention to detail. Although human observers could not see these sections, it was thought that the gods could. Thus, as Mexican archaeologist Eduardo M. Moctezuma points out, "For the Westerner, all the [artistic] work is to be seen. It is a dialogue between humans. For the Aztec in ancient Mexico, it had another character—it was a dialogue with the gods."[32]

Monumental Architecture

Like their statues and other sculptures, the Aztecs' architecture was filled with symbolic qualities that were intended to honor and impress the gods. As for what constitutes architecture, most Aztec houses were small and made of perishable materials; so they are not categorized as architecture. In ancient Mexico, as in ancient Egypt and ancient Greece, architecture is usually defined as monumental—large scale and made of stone or other more permanent materials. Thus, Aztec architecture was primarily confined to the plazas, temples, and other large structures in the ceremonial centers. The central locations of such grand structures served as a type of message because such splendid construction reflected and advertised the military and cultural might of the Aztec Empire.

The chief architectural form in these centers was the temple-pyramid, a truncated (leveled off) pyramid with one or more temples on top. These structures were similar to the pyramids erected by the Maya, Teotihuacanos,

and other earlier Mesoamerican peoples. That is, they were generally rectangular and four sided, with steep staircases on one side and balustrades (stone railings) running along the sides of the steps.

But the Aztec versions were different in some ways. Many had two balustrades or staircases that suddenly changed their slope near the top. Also, some had two staircases. The most famous example was the Templo Mayor in Tenochtitlan, in which each staircase led to one of the twin temples on the summit. In addition, the Aztec Empire featured a few round pyramids, mostly located in the Toluca Valley, lying west of the Valley of Mexico.

Another unusual feature of Aztec temple-pyramids was the common use of overbuilding. When the government decided to build a new temple on the same site as an older one, it did not first tear down the existing one. According to California State University scholar Manuel Aguilar-Moreno:

> Builders would add [the new materials] over the existing edifice. The result would be a new temple that was larger, more extravagant, and more detailed. Enlarging preexisting structures meant adding more stairs and making the sacrificial area more spacious. Layering a preexisting temple was acceptable because the gods had already blessed the original temple; in fact, building a more magnificent temple paid further tribute to the gods.[33]

The most famous example of a pyramid in Aztec culture was the Templo Mayor, shown here. Pyramids were generally four-sided with steep staircases on the sides.

Artistic Crafts

Aztec ceramics (clay pottery) was very high quality and often equal to most medieval European versions. The Aztecs made a large array of practical yet artistically handsome ceramic objects, including bowls, dishes, cups, vases, funerary urns, and incense burners. They also produced numerous items for use in religious rituals, for architectural decoration, and perhaps in some cases, for pure artistic expression.

Among the more striking forms of this art were large, frequently life-size ceramic figures of people and gods. An outstanding example consists of two warriors dressed in eagle outfits, found in the Eagle Temple lying north of the

A performer wears a traditional Aztec feather headdress. Bright feather work was a major craft industry in Aztec society.

Templo Mayor. Eduardo Moctezuma writes:

> These magnificent, life-sized figures were formed in four interlocking sections because of their enormous size. The head, the chest and arms, the abdomen and the thighs, and finally the legs were fitted together to make up these impressive ceramic warriors. The face of the individual inside the bird's head, with its enormous beak, is a brilliant example of Aztec aesthetics [artistic feelings and expression]. The total expression of these figures is not only an example of the extent of utilization of clay the Aztecs achieved, but it [also] succeeds in reproducing the dignity and fierce quality of the warriors of Huitzilopochtli.[34]

Wood carving was another important artistic medium of the Aztecs. The most conspicuous examples are figures of the gods, both large and small, which were painted in bright colors and/or dressed in lavish clothes and jewelry. Other common carved wooden objects include ceremonial masks, shields, spear throwers, drums, and figures of jaguars and other animals. Some sacred wooden artifacts were burned soon after they were created because it was thought that the smoke would rise up into the sky and please certain gods.

The Aztecs also excelled at making jewelry, masks, and other decorative objects with gold and semiprecious stones, such as jade and turquoise.

Making objects with feathers, however, constituted a major craft industry in Aztec-controlled Mexico. Brightly colored bird feathers from numerous different species were used to decorate headdresses, shields, fans, formal clothes, and many other objects. A headdress given to Cortés by the king of Tenochtitlan contained some five hundred magnificent feathers.

Writing, Books, and Literature

The Aztecs were a literate people with a written language and books. All nobles and priests could read, as could a few commoners. A majority of books consisted of long strips of paper that one folded up in a zigzag or accordion-like manner. Such a manuscript was called a codex. (The plural is codices.) Most Aztec paper was made from the inner bark of fig trees, which was first placed in boiling water, then dried out and pounded with a stone hammer.

The Aztec writing system used in these books was the last of five such systems that developed in Mesoamerica. (The earlier ones were Maya, Mixtec, Zapotec, and Epi-Olmec.) Aztec writing consisted of a mixture of pictures and glyphs. The pictures were literal representations of certain objects. The glyphs were picturelike signs that stood for a word, concept, or name. Some glyphs were obvious. For instance, a glyph of a rabbit sitting on a hill meant "on the hill of the rabbit." Concept glyphs, in contrast, required some knowledge of the context of the

Ancient Mexican glyphs. Glyphs are picturelike signs that represent a name, word, or concept.

message or story, as in the case of the glyph depicting a burning temple, which stood for "conquest."

The literature that was produced with this writing system can be conveniently divided into four categories: myths, histories, religious hymns, and poetry. About five hundred codices containing material on these subjects have survived. A majority of them were created directly after the Spanish conquest and were supervised by Spanish priests, so parts of them likely reflect Spanish influences on the natives. Nevertheless, these books reveal much about Aztec ideas and culture.

Particularly noteworthy is surviving Aztec poetry. It mostly reflects aspects of society and life that most people viewed as important or profound in some way. Some poems are based on chants that warriors sang as they headed into battle, for instance. Many others honor the gods or express sor-row over the shortness of life and how mysterious and uncertain life after death is. This beautiful example was purportedly written by the Acolhua king Nezahualcoyotl:

> One day we must go,
>
> one night we will descend into the region of mystery.
>
> Here, we only come to know ourselves;
>
> only in passing are we here on Earth.
>
> In peace and pleasure let us spend our lives; come let us enjoy ourselves.
>
> Let not the angry do so; the Earth is vast indeed!
>
> Would that one lived forever; would that one were not to die![35]

Aztec Scribes

In Aztec society, writing (in books, on animal skins, in paintings, in carved inscriptions, and so forth) was usually the work of a trained individual called a scribe, or tlacuilo, *who could be either a noble or a commoner. The skill and artistic flair of Aztec scribes greatly impressed the Spanish friar Bernadino de Sahagun, who left behind this memory of them:*

The scribe: writings [and] ink [are] his special skills. [He is] a craftsman, an artist, a user of charcoal, a drawer with charcoal, a painter who dissolves colors, grinds pigments, uses colors. The good scribe is honest . . . farsighted [and] a good judge of colors. . . . He paints, applies colors, makes shadows, draws gardens, paints flowers, [and] creates works of art.

Bernadino de Sahagun, *Florentine Codex: General History of the Things of New Spain,* vol. 10, trans. J.O. Anderson and Charles E. Dibble. Santa Fe, NM: School of American Research and University of Utah, 1950, p. 28.

Aztec scribes writing on skins and drawing on the walls.

Aztec Riddles

One of the many important modes of literary expression in Aztec society were riddles, which were often taught in schools. And knowing the answers to riddles was seen as one sign of an educated person. Some surviving Aztec riddles include:

What is a little blue-green jar filled with popcorn? Someone is sure to guess [the answer]. It is the sky.

What is a mountainside that has a spring of water in it? Our nose.

What is that which is a small mirror in a house made of fir branches? Our eye.

What is it that goes along the foothills of the mountain patting our tortillas with its hands? A butterfly.

What is that which we enter in three places and leave by only one? It is our shirt.

What is a tiny colored stone sitting on the road? Dog excrement.

Quoted in Bernadino de Sahagun, *Florentine Codex: General History of the Things of New Spain*, vol. 4, trans. J.O. Anderson and Charles E. Dibble. Santa Fe, NM: School of American Research and University of Utah, 1950, pp. 230–40.

Astronomy and Calendars

Like all ancient peoples, the Aztecs were fascinated by the objects in the night sky, such as the moon, stars, planets, and comets. And their priests and nobles closely followed their nightly, weekly, and yearly movements, seeking to understand how the heavenly bodies and passage of time were connected with the gods and the fate of the world and humanity. Nezahualpilli, a king of Acolhua, was an accomplished astronomer. A Spanish chronicler writes:

[Nezahualpilli] was much concerned with understanding the movement of the celestial bodies. Inclined to the study of these things, he would seek in his kingdom for those who knew of such things, and he would bring them to his court. . . . And at night he would study the stars, and he would go on the roof of his palace, and from there he would watch the stars, and he would discuss [his political and other] problems with them.[36]

The accomplishments of Aztec astronomers are impressive considering that they had no telescopes or other sophisticated equipment. They calculated the length of the solar year by noting where the sun rose on a given morning and counting the number of days (365) until it returned to that same spot. They also laid out both cities and important buildings within them according to astronomical measurements. For example, the Templo Mayor in Tenochtitlan was designed and built so that on the spring equinox (March 21), a person standing directly in front of it would see the sun rise precisely between the twin

An Aztec solar calendar, shown here, was used to keep track of religious observances and ceremonies.

temples at the summit. In addition, Aztec astronomers predicted solar and lunar eclipses and recorded the appearances of comets. In one of his books about the Aztecs, Friar Diego Durán mentions a comet observed by both King Montezuma and King Nezahualpilli:

Having observed the comet since midnight, [Montezuma] went the next day to Nezahualpilli to seek its meaning. [Nezahualpilli replied] "Your vassals, the astronomers, the soothsayers, and diviners have been careless! That sign in the heavens has been there for some time and yet you describe it to me now as it were a new thing. . . . That brilliant [object] appeared in the heavens many days ago."[37]

Also fascinated by time, the Aztecs used several different calendars, largely inherited from earlier Mesoamerican peoples. The main ones were a ritual calendar, an annual calendar, and a 52-year-cycle calendar. The ritual version had 260 days. It was used for keeping track of religious observances and ceremonies, deciding which days were lucky or unlucky, and predicting future events.

A Meaning for Every Activity

Elizabeth H. Boone, a noted scholar of Aztec culture, explains the important influence that the day signs (little pictures that stood for individual days) of the Aztec calendar had on people's everyday lives:

The days [as denoted on the calendar] carried meaning for every activity, and in the Aztec world it was crucial that events happen at the right time. Merchants knew that they should only begin their journeys on a few favorable days: 1 Alligator, 1 Monkey, 7 Serpent, or the best, 1 Serpent, called the "straight way." Approaching home, they would delay on the route to wait for a good day-sign for the homecoming. [The Spanish friar] Father [Diego] Durán was amazed that the Aztecs followed the signs of the days rather than the sign of the fields when it came to the harvest. He recalled how the people would not harvest their corn, even though it was ready and in danger of rotting, until the correct day had arrived. . . . [He] clearly did not understand that timing—doing things according to the [fate-laden signs] of the days—was [to the Aztecs] fundamental to maintaining a balanced world.

Elizabeth H. Boone, *The Aztec World*. Washington, DC: Smithsonian, 1994, p. 115.

Groups or spans of thirteen days within the calendar were thought to have divine symbolic meaning, so each group of thirteen was named for a different god. As modern astrologers do with calendars and birth dates, Aztec priests plugged the birth dates of individuals into the 260-day calendar to predict whether their fates would be fortunate or unfortunate. Unfortunately, some of the many other intricate meanings of the days and numbers that appear in this calendar have been lost over the centuries.

The annual calendar, like most modern ones, was a solar calendar based on the passage of 365 days. The Aztecs used it to keep track of the seasons and various monthly events. They divided each group of twenty days into four weeks of five days each. And they structured their lives around these five-day weeks just as people do today with seven-day weeks. A market that was open for business only one day a week, for instance, was closed for four days.

The 52-year calendar was used to keep track of the years. It was constructed by combining the other two calendars in a complicated mathematical manner. This resulted in a grand cycle of 18,980 days, or 52 years. Each year in a typical cycle had its own number and name, such as 2 Tecpatl, the Aztec version of the European year 1520. Correlating the Aztec and European calendars has allowed modern historians to date many events in late Aztec history with fair precision.

The complexity of the Aztecs' calendars and astronomical record keeping, along with the diversity and high quality of their arts and crafts, demonstrates that they were a thoughtful, accomplished people.

Chapter Five

Weapons and Warfare

Warfare was one of the dominant concerns and enterprises of Aztec civilization. And warrior-oriented themes and institutions were prominent at all levels of society. "An Aztec male's identity was defined by his success in warfare," writes Manuel Aguilar-Moreno, a California State University scholar. Aguilar-Moreno continues:

> Even in female identity, warfare was important. Childbirth was compared to combat. . . . Male education at the telpochcalli schools emphasized military skills and values, and the main aim of [these schools] was to create warriors. Although social status in Aztec society was largely predetermined by family lineage, warfare provided a means of climbing the social ladder. Young warriors elevated their social status by taking captives in bat-

tle, and more important, they secured that status for their descendants.[38]

Indeed, successful warriors enjoyed social status second only to the king and a few high-placed priests and military generals. And these elite fighters were rewarded in numerous ways, according to Friar Diego Durán, who writes:

> They were the men whom the sovereigns most loved and esteemed, the men who obtained most privileges [and] favors, [including] brilliant, splendid weapons and insignia. . . . As soon as the [successful] warrior returned to the [royal] court, the king was informed of the brave deeds of the knight, who was brought before him. [The king] gave him his honor. . . . The hair on top of his head was parted in two, and a red cord wrapped around it. In the same

cord was attached an ornament of green, blue, and red feathers.[39]

Preparing for War

The objective of the wars Aztec warriors fought was not, as was often the case in Europe, to acquire new territories and human subjects to rule. Indeed, most towns and peoples the Aztecs conquered were allowed to keep their local leaders, governments, and customs. The chief aim of these wars was to achieve domination over the conquered peoples so that they would be forced to pay tribute to the Aztec king and homeland. In this way, the Aztecs were assured of a steady inflow of foodstuffs, cloth, weapons, building materials, pa-

per, feathers and other decorative items, and so forth.

The decision to go to war rested with the king, likely after consulting with his closest advisers. Once that decision was made, he turned to his chief generals, who helped to plan and organize the military campaign, which was a large and complex undertaking. One of their first acts was to call on large numbers of Aztec men to temporarily leave their occupations and become soldiers. Per custom, those men who had fought and distinguished themselves in prior wars were given gifts, including handsome shields and special uniforms.

Women were not as a rule recruited as soldiers. However, when their community or home was under direct attack,

Aztec warriors engaging one another to prepare for battle.

they fought with great valor alongside the men. Also, women were sometimes used in strategic ways by kings and generals. When the Spanish were laying siege to Tenochtitlan, for example, at one point the king had most of the women stand on the rooftops and shout threats at the attackers. According to Friar Durán, "When Cortés saw the great number of people covering the flat roofs and filling the streets of the city, he became afraid and feared that he would not be able to conquer Mexico."[40]

The preparations for achieving domination over a foreign people, an endeavor that might or might not involve actual fighting, were highly ritualized, with set rules and procedures. First, the Aztec king sent out ambassadors, who requested that the enemy surrender peacefully. If this demand was refused, the Aztecs sent threats that warned of dire consequences, including death and destruction. Only if the threats were ineffective did the Aztec king order the soldiers to assemble and prepare to attack.

Offensive Weapons

The warriors who marched toward their confrontation with the enemy carried a wide array of effective weapons, with which they were highly skilled. One of the more dependable and deadly of these tools of war was the atlatl. A kind of throwing stick, it was roughly 18 inches (46cm) long and consisted of a wooden handle with a groove. The warrior placed a dart or short spear inside the groove and then fired the weapon by flipping the stick

in a forceful overhand motion. The atlatl gave the spear more power than was possible to achieve by throwing with the arm alone. It was also effective because the warrior could fire it with one hand. That allowed him to keep an enemy at bay with one arm while he aided a wounded comrade with the other arm.

The atlatl was quite lethal in battle for another reason. The Aztecs (and other

An atlatl was a deadly tool of war for the Aztecs.

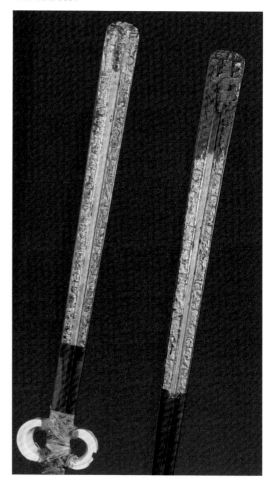

Native Archers and Their Equipment

Although the atlatl was a key missile weapon for Mesoamerican warriors, including Aztec fighters, they also used bows and arrows. The bows, which were made of hickory or ash wood, varied in size, the largest measuring about 5 feet (1.5m) long. Bowstrings were typically made from deerskin twisted into a thong or from animal sinew (tendon). Arrows were fashioned from river reeds strengthened with plant fibers and tipped by points carved from fishbone, flint, or obsidian. In battle, as in hunting, warriors kept a supply of arrows in a quiver made of leather or some other flexible material. Aztec archers were often extremely skilled. The Spanish soldier Bernal Diaz del Castillo, who accompanied Cortés to Mexico, reported that they could fire two arrows at a time with amazing accuracy. It is unclear how far these native archers could fire an arrow. But modern experiments with replicas of their bows suggest the range was 300–600 feet (91m–183m).

Mesoamericans) learned to use it at a young age and practiced consistently for many years. In fact, the average Aztec was more adept at using an atlatl than an average European soldier was at wielding a sword. As a result, many Spaniards were mightily impressed by native employment of the atlatl. A Spanish soldier who witnessed the weapon in battle in the 1540s said, "[This formidable weapon] is capable of sending a dart with such great force that it has been seen to pass completely through a man armed with a coat of [armor]."[41]

Other missile, or projectile, weapons used by the Aztecs included the spear, the bow and arrow, and various kinds of slings (*tematlatl*). The slings fired smooth stones as far as 660 feet (201m), doing considerable damage. One awed

Spaniard later recalled, "I have seen a stone shot from a sling break a sword in two when it was held in a man's hand thirty yards away."[42]

Aztec soldiers also used swords, the most common example being the maquauhuitl. Unlike Spanish swords, which were made of steel, the maquauhuitl had razor-sharp slices of stone, most often obsidian. There were two kinds of maquauhuitl—a one-handed version and a two-handed version. The one-handed one was about 3 feet (1m) long; the two-handed version was about 5 feet (1.5m) long. Each resembled a club, except that it had grooves on its sides, into which slices of stone were wedged. One of Cortés's men saw an Aztec warrior with a maquauhuitl confront a mounted

Spaniard and later wrote that the sword "struck the horse in the chest, cutting through to the inside and killing the horse on the spot." That same day, he "saw another Indian give a horse a sword thrust in the neck that laid the horse dead at his feet."[43]

Defensive Gear

Supplementing the Aztecs' array of offensive weapons were various defensive devices, chief among them shields, or *yaochimalli*. They were made from several different materials, including wood, woven cane, split bamboo, and animal hides (or sometimes a combination of some of these). The warriors frequently decorated their shields with paint, feathers, and/or carvings of animals. Eyewitness testimony from Europeans indicates that the native shields were highly effective on the battlefield. One Spaniard said, "The shields are so strong that only a good crossbow can shoot through them, but arrows [from an ordinary bow] do not damage them."[44]

Further protection was afforded by helmets and armor. (The Aztecs did not fight naked, as incorrectly depicted in some modern books and movies.) The helmets were constructed of wood, animal bone, or bone covered by a layer of wood or quilted cotton. Some warriors used large, intact animal skulls as helmets and gazed outward through the opened jaw.

The most common form of body armor, called *ichcahuipilli*, was fashioned from wads of raw cotton stuffed between layers of cloth. This armor was often two fingers thick and was almost as good as European chain mail in protecting a warrior. Some suits of native armor—usually those of nobles or highly accomplished warriors—had thick outer layers of feathers. These provided extra protection as well as announced the wearer's high status and personal pride.

Armies in Action

The warriors' atlatls, bows, slings, swords, shields, and armor were made even more formidable looking by the colorful insignia and body paint these fighters wore. The insignia, which indicated rank or status, included feathers and other handsome decorations. They were most often attached to helmets and shields. Body paint was also used as a kind of insignia, as in the case of a warrior who painted his face yellow and red because he had once captured an enemy soldier. Other soldiers painted their bodies black and/or covered their faces with black stripes. Many Spaniards found the combination of Aztec arms, armor, and insignia an awesome sight. One Spanish soldier remarked, "It is one of the most beautiful sights in the world to see them in their battle array."[45]

This stunningly attired native army was organized into basic platoon-like units of twenty men each. In various situations, these combined into larger, company- or squad-like units of four hundred men. The larger unit was led by an officer called a *tiachcauh*, who hailed from the same town or neighborhood his men did. Above him were officers with titles such as "chief of men" and "chief of the house of arrows."

As the officers and their men marched along, the king sent out spies (*quimichtin*) to gather intelligence about the enemy. These men carefully dressed like the enemy and spoke his language. Sometimes the spies were able to determine when and where the opposing forces would camp and make their stand against the approaching Aztecs.

Eventually the two armies confronted each other. Battles usually took place in the morning, shortly after dawn. The Aztec king or leading general drew up his men in long lines, and when he felt the time was right, he ordered groups of archers and slingers to begin launching their missiles. Once he judged that the enemy had been softened up, he signaled to some priests, who blew shell trumpets to initiate the infantry charge. "When the priests blew them," a European witness recalled, the warriors "as one arose [and] war cries were raised."[46] The foot soldiers surged forward, smashed into the enemy lines, and swung away with their deadly stone-bladed swords.

A typical battle lasted at least an hour and in some cases dragged on for several. Engaging in hand-to-hand combat for such long periods was obviously exhausting. And it was common practice for a tired soldier to temporarily withdraw and rest while a fresh soldier took his place. The combination of stamina, fighting skill, and sheer courage possessed by many Aztec warriors was a

An Aztec warrior with an atlatl, decorated shield and armor, and face paint.

A Spaniard Describes Native Armor

A surviving account by an anonymous Spanish soldier includes an informative description of the armor used by the Aztecs and other Mesoamericans:

The armor they use in warfare [is made] of quilted cotton the thickness of a finger and a half and sometimes two fingers, which is very strong. Over these they wear suits all of one piece and of a heavy cloth, which they tie in the back. These are covered with feathers of different colors. . . . The strength of their feathered garments is proportionate to their weapons, so that they resist spears and arrows, and even the sword. To defend the head, they wear [helmets] of wood, covered on the outside with feathers [or] gold or precious stones, and are something wonderful to see.

Quoted in Patricia de Fuentes, ed., *The Conquistadors: First-Person Accounts of the Conquest of Mexico*. Norman: University of Oklahoma Press, 1993, pp. 168–69.

sight to behold according to several Spanish eyewitnesses. One wrote:

Among them are extraordinarily brave men who face death with absolute determination. I saw one of them defend himself courageously against two swift horses, and another against three and four, and when the Spanish horsemen could not kill him, one of the horsemen in desperation hurled his lance, which the Indian caught in the air, and fought with him for more than an hour. . . . During combat they sing and dance and sometimes give the wildest shouts and whistles imaginable, especially when they know they have the advantage. Anyone facing them for the first time can be terrified by their screams and their ferocity.[47]

The Aftermath of Battle

Although the warriors did their best to kill and maim opposing soldiers, the main objective was to capture at least some of them. The more captives a soldier took, the higher his military rank and social status would rise. After the battle was over, an officer called the "master of the captives" settled any disputes over who had captured whom. And in the days that followed, the soldiers with confirmed captures received their rewards. These included lavish insignia; expensive capes and other clothes; stores of food, including chocolate; and other items deemed valuable.

The elevation of a captor's personal status was not the only reason that taking war captives was important to the Aztecs. A certain number of live prisoners were also necessary to appease the war god, Huitzilopochtli. Most of the captives were bound and marched back to Tenochtitlan, where they were taken to that god's temple and sacrificed.

Another important issue following an Aztec victory was what should be done about the defeated enemy. In most cases, the enemy was so crippled and demoralized that its leader immediately acknowledged defeat and agreed to pay the Aztec king tribute. As long as the tribute was paid on a regular basis,

the defeated leader and his advisers were allowed to retain their authority over their own people.

On occasion, however, an enemy defeated in battle refused to pay. In such a case, the Aztec king usually ordered his army to march to the enemy capital and intimidate its inhabitants by its mere presence. If this did not work, the next step was to destroy one or more of the temples in that city. For Mesoamerican peoples, this constituted a devastating loss and almost always resulted in submission. (This is why the Aztec glyph meaning "conquest" consists of an image of a burning temple.) Only extremely rarely did a defeated people

The Aztec god of war Huitzilopochtli. Captured prisoners of war were often sacrificed to the god after battle.

"A Sight to See"

The Spanish historian Francisco Lopez de Gomara, a contemporary of Cortés, penned this description of the native army that confronted Cortés and his men when they first entered Tlaxcalan territory in September 1519:

The men were splendidly armed in their fashion and their faces were painted with red [body paint], which gave them the look of devils. They carried plumes and maneuvered marvelously well. Their weapons were slings, pikes, lances, swords, and bows and arrows; helmets; arm and leg armor of wood, gilded or covered with feathers or leather. Their breastplates were of cotton. Their shields [which were] very handsome and not at all weak, were of tough wood and leather, with brass and feather ornaments. Their swords [were] of wood with [pieces of sharpened] flint set into them, which cut well and made a nasty wound. Their troops were arranged in squadrons, each with many trumpets, conches [seashells], and drums, all of which was a sight to see.

Quoted in Hammond Innes, *The Conquistadors*. New York: Knopf, 1969, p. 81.

remain defiant after losing its temple (or temples); in such a case, the Aztec king felt he had no other choice but to destroy the entire enemy capital.

These were the various customs and results of warfare before the Aztecs suddenly learned that Mesoamerica was not the center of a world inhabited only by Native Americans. In 1519 they were jolted into the realization that other lands existed across the great seas. Moreover, the light-skinned residents of those lands possessed weapons and strange beasts (horses) that the Aztecs had never dreamed of. The nature of warfare in Mesoamerica was about to change. And this time it would be the people of Tenochtitlan who would endure the agony of seeing their temples destroyed.

Chapter Six

The Arrival of the Spanish

Throughout most of his seventeen-year reign, Montezuma II, ruler of the vast Aztec Empire, had no inkling that he would be the last king of his people. Nor did he imagine that his mighty realm would soon be transformed from a living reality into a memory of past glories. Yet these were the destinies that history was about to confer on them.

When the story of the Aztecs' fall was told and retold in the years immediately following the conquest, there was much talk of fate. Accounts written in both Nahuatl and Spanish describe strange omens, divine signs that appeared before the Spaniards arrived and warned that dire events would soon occur. Ten years before they arrived, one account claims, one of these omens suddenly appeared in the sky: "It was like a flaming ear of corn, or a fiery signal, or the blaze of daybreak. It seemed to bleed fire, drop by drop, like a wound in the sky." Another

omen took the form of a giant lightning bolt that struck a temple of the fire god Xiuhtecuhtli. Seeing it, some people reportedly exclaimed, "The temple was struck by a blow from the sun!" Still another divine warning was remembered as a weeping woman who haunted Tenochtitlan night after night, saying, "My children, we must flee far away from this city!"[48]

In retrospect, it is difficult to tell how much truth there is in these supposed omens. Some may have been based on real events. The "flaming ear of corn" in the sky, for instance, may well have been a comet observed by Aztec astronomers. But modern scholars think that efforts to interpret these events as predictions of an oncoming catastrophe came only after the fact. It was difficult for the surviving Aztecs to accept that the destruction of their civilization could be accomplished by mere mortals like themselves. So they searched for evidence, in the form of strange past events, that indicated the gods had ordained this calamity. This was a concept they could readily understand. After all, their religious and historical writings had long foretold that the world they lived in was ordained by the gods to end in disaster.

The Majestic Montezuma

In the years immediately preceding the conquest, the Aztec Empire was strong and prosperous. And its leader enjoyed enormous authority, prestige, and respect. Montezuma II had been thirty-four when he had ascended the throne in 1502. So in the year the Spanish arrived, 1519, he was fifty-one. The Spanish chronicler Bernal Diaz del Castillo, who met him, wrote that the Aztec king was tall, slender, and muscular, as well as clean-cut and always dressed in fresh, handsome clothing. One sign of Montezuma's great power, Diaz del Castillo said, was the size and splendor of his daily meals, overseen by a small army of cooks and servants. He explains:

> They daily cooked fowl, turkeys, pheasants, native partridges, quail, tame and wild ducks, venison [deer], wild boar, reed birds, pigeons, hares and rabbits, and many sorts of birds and other things which are bred in this country, and they are so numerous that I cannot finish naming them in a hurry.[49]

Another description of Montezuma at the height of his power comes from the unknown Spanish author of *Codex Mendoza*, who writes:

> [He was] skilled in all arts, civil as well as military. His subjects greatly respected him [and] none of his predecessors, in comparison, could approach his great state and majesty. [In addition] he was so greatly feared by his vassals, and by his captains and leaders, that when they negotiated with him out of the great esteem and fear that they had, none dared look him in the face.[50]

The surviving Aztec historical records show that during his long reign Montezuma engaged in numerous conquests. He also put down several rebellions among the empire's subject peoples. Thus, by 1519 he had become a supremely confident and accomplished individual. However, history shows that he was completely unprepared for the arrival of strange men from across the ocean.

The first reports about these strangers that reached Montezuma came from people who lived near the eastern seashore. They told him they had seen "two towers or small mountains floating on the waves of the sea." Men had climbed out of these towers into a small boat and begun "fishing with hooks and lines." One messenger told Montezuma:

> They fished until late and then they went back to their two great towers and climbed up into them. There

Montezuma II was greatly respected by his subjects but ill prepared for the arrival of the Spanish.

were about fifteen of these people, some with blue jackets, others with red, [and] they have very light skin, much lighter than ours. They all have long beards, and their hair comes only to their ears.[51]

No one knows for sure what Montezuma and his advisers thought about the strangers' sudden appearance. One often-cited account suggests that they suspected it was the return of Quetzalcoatl, a legendary figure from the period before the Aztecs had settled in the Valley of Mexico. A human ruler who was an earthly manifestation of the god by that same name, Quetzalcoatl had supposedly been light-skinned and bearded. The legends claimed that he had eventually departed Mexico and vanished over the eastern horizon after promising to return some day. According to a surviving Aztec story, Montezuma believed that Quetzalcoatl had indeed returned. "He has appeared!" the king reportedly shouted. "He has come back! He will come here, to the place of his throne . . . for that is what he promised when he departed!"[52]

The Adventurous Cortés

Although it is possible that Montezuma actually thought he was witnessing the return of a semidivine figure, it is equally possible that this story was manufactured later. Some scholars point out that it came from a Spanish account written several decades after the conquest. In their view, the natives whom the author interviewed may

have wanted to explain away and excuse Montezuma's failure to stop the Spanish onslaught. The idea that he sincerely believed that Cortés was Quetzalcoatl and that Cortés took advantage of this honest mistake made Mon-

This Aztec drawing shows the route taken by Spanish conquistador Hernán Cortés from the east coast of Mexico to Tenochtitlan.

The People in the Mirror

Of the omens that supposedly warned the preconquest Aztecs that something bad was going to befall them in the near future, one was said to show images of warlike people riding on top of animals, supposedly a premonition of the Spanish riding horses. A native account of the omen says:

A strange creature was captured in the nets. The men who fish the lakes caught a bird the color of ashes [and] brought it to Montezuma. . . . The bird wore a strange mirror in the crown of its head. The mirror was pierced in the center like a spindle whorl, and the night sky could be seen in its face. The hour was noon, but the stars . . . could be seen in the face of that mirror. [When Montezuma] looked at the mirror a second time, he saw a distant plain. People were moving across it, spread out in ranks and coming forward in great haste. They made war against each other and rose on the backs of animals resembling deer.

Quoted in Miguel Leon-Portilla, *The Broken Spears: The Aztec Account of the Conquest of Mexico.* Boston: Beacon, 1992, p. 6.

tezuma a more sympathetic and tragic character.

Whatever the Aztec ruler actually thought about the strangers from the east, it is documented that he sent messengers bearing gifts to meet them. This turned out to be a mistake because the newcomers' motivations were neither friendly nor civil. What Montezuma did not then know was that Cortés and his men were from a distant land called Spain. Born there in 1484, Cortés had fought in wars in southern Spain and Italy as a young man. Seeking adventure and wealth, he sailed to the new Spanish colony on the island of Hispaniola in the East Indies in 1506. Three years later he moved to Cuba, another Spanish-ruled island. And by cattle ranching, he fulfilled his dream of becoming rich.

Yet Cortés still craved adventure and even greater wealth. And to satisfy these yearnings, in 1518 he involved himself in an upcoming expedition to the then-mysterious Mexican mainland. Cuba's Spanish governor, Diego Velázquez, put Cortés in command of the venture. In February 1519, the expedition departed Cuba in eleven ships with 530 European soldiers and other personnel, several hundred Cuban Indians and Africans, a few dozen handheld guns (primitive front loaders called harquebuses), nearly twenty cannons, sixteen horses, and many large dogs trained for warfare.

Cortés first explored the coast of the Yucatán Peninsula, which was then inhabited by Mayan natives who were not subject to the Aztec king. After making some brief initial contacts, the Spanish sailed northward around the Yucatán to the mouth of the Tabasco River.

Going ashore, they encountered some natives who were Aztec subjects. These locals gave the newcomers a hostile reception and, when they did not leave, attacked them. One of Cortés's soldiers later described the small-scale battle, which the Spanish handily won: "[Cortés] ordered us to fire the guns [and] a few of us were wounded . . . but at last the speed of our attack . . . drove them out of the village, [which] we took [and] occupied."[53]

Awed by the Spaniards' guns and fighting ability, the natives suddenly welcomed them and gave them gifts, including servants. One of those servants turned out to be of great benefit to Cortés. Called Malinche, she became his mistress and he took her everywhere he went thereafter. In his eyes, one of her major assets was that she spoke fluent Nahuatl, which meant that she would be able to translate for him when he eventually confronted the Aztec leaders. (She quickly learned Spanish to help with her translations.)

The March on Tenochtitlan

Montezuma's messengers found the Spanish not long after their small skirmish with the natives along the coast. Speaking through Malinche, the messengers told Cortés that their mighty ruler, Montezuma, had heard about the strangers' arrival and wanted to offer them food and shelter. The Spaniards accepted these gifts. They also took the time to demonstrate their military power by firing their cannons. Cortés's motive was to instill fear in the messengers, and it worked because they fainted and fell to the ground. After they had been revived, they headed home to Tenochtitlan and told Montezuma about the marvels they had seen. Describing the cannon, one messenger said:

> A thing like a ball of stone comes out of its entrails [guts]. It comes out shooting sparks and raining fire. The smoke that comes out with it has a pestilent [deadly] odor, like that of rotten mud. . . . If the cannon is aimed against a mountain, the mountain splits and cracks open. If it is aimed against a tree, it shatters the tree into splinters.[54]

The messengers also told the king about the Spaniards' iron swords and armor, light-colored skin, and long beards. Astounded by this account, Montezuma had his spies keep a close watch on the Spanish and their activities in the weeks that followed.

Because he was having them watched, the Aztec king knew when the Spanish began marching inland in the direction of the Valley of Mexico.

One surviving native description of the approaching foreign army reads:

> [The Spaniards] came grouped, they came assembled, they came raising dust. Their iron lances [and other weapons] seemed to glisten [and] some came all in iron. They came [having been] turned into iron. They came gleaming. Hence they [marched

Cortés, seated at center, meets with Aztec emissaries. Malinche, standing next to Cortés, was his trusted translator.

Xaltelolco.

along] causing great astonishment. Hence they [marched] causing great fear.⁵⁵

Montezuma was particularly disturbed when word came that Cortés had entered the valley of the Tlaxcalans, the only local people the Aztecs had not yet conquered. Hearing that the Tlaxcalans despised the Aztecs, the Spanish commander offered to forge an alliance. The Tlaxcalans expressed interest in this idea, although they bargained shrewdly. First, the Tlaxcalan leader said, the Spanish must help them fight another local enemy, the residents of Cholula, a city lying thirty miles to the south. Cortés agreed to the deal. And not long afterward his men took part in a gruesome massacre of several thousand Cholulans.

"The Spaniards and Indians in our company went out in squads to different parts of the city, killing warriors and burning houses," one of Cortés's officers later recalled.⁵⁶

"They Hungered Like Pigs"

Following the bloody event in Cholula, the Spaniards and their newly acquired native allies moved on toward Tenochtitlan. They had not gone far when more messengers from Montezuma approached. They offered Cortés a number of exquisite gifts, including gold necklaces and quantities of brightly colored feathers. Apparently they expected the Spaniards to accept these offerings as a good-will gesture and then turn around and return to their ships.

Earlier Spanish Explorers in Mexico

Cortés's expedition was not the first Spanish foray into Mexico. In 1517 a Cuban Spaniard named Francisco Hernandez de Cordoba landed with 110 men on the coast of the Yucatán Peninsula, where he encountered some local Maya. Some of these people attacked him and the Spanish incurred heavy losses, so Cordoba returned to Cuba. In April of the following year, another Spaniard, Juan de Grijalva, also sailed to the Yucatán and suffered military casualties. But before departing, he spoke to some of the Maya and they informed him that a large city existed in the center of a great lake lying many miles inland. That city, they said, was the capital of a mighty empire that held sway over many peoples, including some of the Maya. Grijalva became convinced that the rulers of that native empire were wealthy with gold and other valuables. And that was a major incentive for other Spaniards, including Cortés, to organize new expeditions to explore and exploit Mexico.

But this was a vain hope. One of the primary reasons that Cortés and his men had come to Mexico was to get their hands on gold and other valuables. And seeing these glittering gifts only whetted their appetites for more riches. According to one native account:

> When they were given these presents, the Spaniards burst into smiles. Their eyes shone with pleasure [and] they picked up the gold and fingered it like monkeys. . . . The truth is that they longed and lusted for gold. Their bodies swelled with greed [and] they hungered like pigs for that gold.[57]

In the days that followed, Montezuma and his advisers argued over what should be done about the approaching strangers. It appears that some Aztec leaders believed the Spanish were gods previously unknown to the Aztecs. So they should be welcomed. Other advisers argued that the strangers were nothing more than ordinary men who had come to conquer and loot. Why else would they ally themselves with the Aztecs' chief enemy? One adviser warned the king: "I pray to our gods that you will not let the strangers into your house. They will cast you out of it and overthrow your rule, and when you try to recover what you have lost, it will be too late."[58]

Messengers sent from Montezuma offered Cortés many gifts, including feathers and jewelry, to try to maintain peace.

But Montezuma did not agree with this ominous prophecy. He decided that the best course of action was to welcome the newcomers as friends. After all, he confidently told his advisers, if the Spanish did turn out to be hostile, he could always order his warriors to destroy them.

Promises of Friendship

Thus, the Aztecs at first offered no resistance when Cortés and his followers arrived at the southern shore of Lake Texcoco in early November 1519. The Spaniards, who could see Tenochtitlan in the distance, were amazed by its great size and beauty. One of Cortés's soldiers later wrote:

> The circumference of this city is from two and a half to three leagues [8 miles, or 13km]. Most of the persons who have seen it judge it to have sixty thousand inhabitants or more. [The city] has many beautiful and wide streets [and] very beautiful squares [and] many beautiful houses belonging to the [Aztec] lords.[59]

The Spanish reached the city's entrance by marching over a 5-mile (8km) -long stone causeway. Thousands of people gathered on rooftops to catch a glimpse of the strange visitors from a faraway land. A group of Aztec officials exited the gate, approached Cortés, and greeted him in Nahuatl. Malinche, who stood beside Cortés, dutifully translated.

Then Montezuma appeared, clad in his most resplendent clothes and jewelry. He walked to Cortés and placed a golden necklace around his neck. The Spaniard then returned the favor, putting a string of painted beads around the king's neck. At this point, Cortés asked, "Are you Montezuma? Are you the king?" And Montezuma answered, "Yes, I am Montezuma." Moving closer to Cortés, he added, "You are weary.

The Aztecs welcomed Cortés and his troops when they arrived in Tenochtitlan.

Ode to the Greatest City

Of the many songs composed by the Aztecs, some were patriotic odes, comparable to American songs like "America the Beautiful." The following surviving example expresses pride in the Aztec capital of Tenochtitlan, which the composer perceives as invincible:

Proud of itself is the city of Mexico-Tenochtitlan. Here, no one fears to die in war. This is our glory. This is Your Command, O Giver of Life! [a reference to the creator-god, Ometeotl] Have this in mind, O princes [of rival cities and lands], [and] do not forget it. Who could [ever] conquer Tenochtitlan? Who could shake the foundation of the heavens?

Quoted in Miguel Leon-Portilla, *Pre-Columbian Literatures of Mexico*. Norman: University of Oklahoma Press, 1969, p. 87.

The journey has tired you, but now you have arrived on the Earth." After Malinche had translated, Cortés told her, "Tell Montezuma that we are his friends. There is nothing to fear. We have wanted to see him for a long time, and now we have seen his face and heard his words. Tell him that we love him well and that our hearts are contented."[60]

These words spoken by Cortés were lies, of course. Far from being Montezuma's friends, the Spanish had come, just as the king's adviser had warned, to conquer and plunder. As history would show, the moment the Spanish entered Tenochtitlan, that city and the great empire it ruled were doomed.

Chapter Seven

Fall of the Aztec Empire

The tranquil talk of friendship between Montezuma and Cortés was short lived. Having achieved his goal of making it into the Aztec capital without a fight, the Spanish leader decided not to waste too much time on meaningless niceties. And on November 16, 1519, about a week after the Spanish arrival, he ordered Montezuma's arrest. The alleged reason for this audacious move was that some Aztecs had attacked some Spaniards near the Atlantic coast. The real motive, of course, was that Cortés wanted to give the orders in Tenochtitlan. Still, for a while he did so indirectly, making it look as if Montezuma was still in charge while forcing the captive king to do Cortés's bidding.

The first demand Cortés made on his hostage was to reveal the whereabouts of the royal treasure storehouses. Feeling he had no choice, and perhaps naively thinking that the Spanish would leave if they were given enough

gold, Montezuma led them to the first storehouse. Spanish soldiers "surrounded him and crowded close with their weapons," according to a surviving native account. "He walked in the center, while they formed a circle around him." After looting this treasure trove, they moved on to another. The account continues:

When they entered, it was if they [the Spaniards] had arrived in Paradise. They searched everywhere and covered everything. They were slaves to their own greed. All of Montezuma's possessions were brought out, [including] fine bracelets, necklaces with large stones, ankle rings with little gold bells, the royal crowns and all the royal finery—everything that belonged to the king and was reserved to him only. They seized these treasures as if they were their own, as if this plunder was merely a stroke of good luck. And when they had taken all the gold, they heaped up everything else in the middle of the patio.[61]

At the time, Montezuma did not fully grasp that this was only the beginning of the Spaniards' demands and outrages. Moreover, it is likely that he still underestimated their abilities. He probably continued to hold out hope that his warriors and empire were too strong for such a small group of interlopers to overcome. But this would soon prove to be a fatal error in judgment.

A week after the Spanish arrived they turned on the Aztecs, ordered the arrest of Montezuma, and took control of Tenochtitlan.

Fighting Erupts in the City

The realization that the intruders were not merely thieves, but also mass murderers, became plain to Montezuma in April 1520, a few months into his captivity. Cortés suddenly took some of his soldiers and hurried off to the coast. (He did not explain to his royal prisoner that representatives of the Spanish government in Cuba had come to arrest Cortés for committing various acts without its approval; and he was planning to ambush them.) Before departing, Cortés left his second in command, Pedro de Alvarado, in charge of Tenochtitlan.

Like Cortés, Alvarado believed that the Aztecs were savages. Also, because they were non-Christians, he saw them as misguided inferiors who must be forced to accept and respect what the Spanish viewed as the one true god. For these reasons, he saw nothing wrong with brutalizing and killing as many natives as it took to establish Spanish superiority, control, and religious conversion.

These may have been Alvarado's motives for ordering a sneak attack on thousands of unarmed dancers and singers who were taking part in the annual Festival of Toxcatl. This large-scale ceremony was dedicated to Tezcatlipoca, the god seen as a punisher of the wicked, but also as a patron of

The Capital's General Layout

In preparing to lay siege to Tenochtitlan, Cortés had the advantage of having spent many months there. So he knew the layout and could formulate effective strategies for attacking or aiming his cannons at specific sections. The renowned Mexican archaeologist Eduardo M. Moctezuma, who has spent years reconstructing what the original city looked like, here briefly describes its general layout:

Starting in the center, formed by the ceremonial precinct of Tenochtitlan with its seventy-eight buildings, mostly temples, we see the great causeways running [away across the lake] toward the cardinal directions. Just outside the [central] ceremonial precinct were located the palaces of the great lords. . . . Farther from the main ceremonial center [were] the capullis [residential neighborhoods] with their local temples and the houses of their traditional [leaders] and the simple houses of the [commoners].

Quoted in Eduardo M. Moctezuma, "Aztec History and Cosmovision," in *Moctezuma's Mexico: Visions of the Aztec World*, by David Carrasco and Eduardo M. Moctezuma. Niwot: University Press of Colorado, 1992, pp. 72, 74.

beauty and kingship. Each spring, a young man (usually a war captive) was chosen to impersonate the god for a year. Priests dressed him in fine clothes, supplied him with the best foods, and assigned him several wives. The following spring, these same priests sacrificed him to Tezcatlipoca by cutting out his heart. The Aztecs believed that this gory act, accompanied by dancing, singing, and other festivities, was necessary to satisfy the god.

Alvarado seems to have felt that such open and lavish adoration of what he saw as a false god could not be tolerated. So at the height of the celebration he gave the go-ahead for a major assault. The Spanish soldiers "ran in among the dancers, forcing their way to the place where the drums were played," according to a surviving account. The account also states:

> They attacked the man who was drumming and cut off his arms. Then they cut off his head and it rolled across the floor. They attacked all the celebrants, stabbing them, spearing them, striking them with their swords. They attacked some of them from behind and these fell instantly to the ground with their entrails hanging out. Others they beheaded [or] split their heads to pieces [or] slashed others in the abdomen and their entrails all spilled to the ground. Some attempted to run away, but their intestines dragged as they ran [and] no matter how they tried to save themselves, they could find no escape.... The blood of the warriors flowed like water and gathered into pools. The pools widened and the stench of blood and entrails filled the air.[62]

The massacre confused and horrified the Aztecs. They had always followed strict rules about warfare, and their bloodletting, both on the battlefield and in temple sacrifices, was highly ritualized. Attacking and killing unarmed people in the midst of religious worship was something they had never conceived of and could not understand. It is not surprising, therefore, that they rose up and tried to expel the Spanish from the city. According to a native account:

> The captains assembled at once. They all carried their spears and shields. Then the battle began. The Aztecs attacked with javelins and arrows, even with the light spears that are used for hunting birds. They hurled their javelins with all their strength and the cloud of missiles spread out over the Spaniards like a yellow cloak. The Spaniards immediately took refuge in the palace. They began to shoot at the Mexica with their iron arrows and to fire their cannons and arquebuses [primitive guns].[63]

The Aztecs Retaliate

A few days later Cortés returned (having won his battle on the coast) and was appalled to find that the soldiers he had left behind were trapped in Montezuma's palace. To keep those men from escaping, the Aztecs had dismantled some bridges and installed heavy guards on the others. Cortés now tried to go on the offensive but could make little headway, as he said in a letter he later penned to the Spanish king:

I sallied forth at two or three different points, where they were engaged stoutly with our men. And at

one time, when a captain had led forth 200 men, they fell upon them before he had time to form them in order, and killed four of their number, besides wounding the captain and several others. I was also

wounded, and many of the Spaniards who were with me engaged in another quarter. We destroyed few of the enemy, because they took refuge beyond the bridges, and did us much injury from the roofs of houses and terraces, some of which fell into our possession and were burned. But they were so numerous and strong, and so well defended and supplied with stones and other arms, that our whole force was not sufficient to take them, nor to prevent the enemy from attacking us at their pleasure.[64]

The Spanish were now at such a disadvantage that Cortés turned to Montezuma for help. The captive monarch was told he must order his angry people to fall back and put down their arms. Montezuma attempted to do so. But seeing him as a pawn of the intruders, most Aztecs no longer trusted or respected him, and they threw rocks at him, forcing him back into the palace. A sad consequence of this incident was that Montezuma was no longer useful to the Spanish. So Cortés ordered that the king and all the Aztec nobles then in Spanish custody be strangled to death and that their bodies be thrown into a courtyard adjacent to the palace. A Spanish eyewitness later recalled how that night a large group of women carrying torches entered the courtyard:

Montezuma pleaded with his people not to fight the Spanish. When his plea failed, the Spanish killed him.

They came for their husbands and relatives who lay dead [and] they came for Montezuma, too. And as the women recognized their men . . . they threw themselves upon them with great sorrow and grief, and raised such a wailing and crying that it filled one with fear. I was on guard duty then, and I said to my companion, "Have you not seen hell [over there]? For if you have not seen it, you may witness it from here."[65]

Cortés soon found to his dismay that the murder of Montezuma and his nobles had been a major blunder. Although the Aztecs had lost confidence in their king, they considered his brutal murder the final outrage. And it became clear to Cortés that a full-scale attack by tens of thousands of warriors and townspeople was about to occur. Realizing it would be suicide for the small force of Spaniards to remain in the city, he ordered a hasty and if possible quiet retreat. In the middle of the night on July 1, 1520, they stealthily climbed onto a causeway and began making their way toward the shore. Some of the Aztecs saw what was happening, however, and raised an alarm. Thousands of warriors converged on the causeway, where a furious battle ensued. More than six hundred of Cortés's men were killed, many of whom were weighted down with treasure that they refused to leave behind. Spanish writers later came to call the event the Noche Triste, or "Night of Sorrows."

Cortés Returns

Having driven the hated intruders out of Tenochtitlan, the Aztecs attempted to regroup and rebuild. Thousands of people worked to restore ruined houses and reconstruct the bridges that had been dismantled. Also, the surviving nobles chose a new king—Cuitlahuac, one of the advisers who had counseled Montezuma not to allow the Spanish into the city.

But as it turned out, although the Spanish soldiers had gone away, they had left behind another army, an invisible one that now wreaked havoc on the Aztec capital and nearby regions. Unknowingly, the Spanish had brought smallpox with them to Mexico. In the weeks that followed, the disease spread with terrifying swiftness through the native population, which had no natural resistance to it. "Sores erupted on our faces, our breasts, our bellies," a native writer attested. He added:

We were covered with agonizing sores from head to foot. The illness was so dreadful that no one could walk or move. The sick were so utterly helpless that they could only lie on their beds like corpses [and] if they did move their bodies they screamed with pain. A great many died from this plague, and many others died of hunger. They could not get up to search for food, and everyone else was too sick to care for them, so they starved to death in their beds.[66]

The onset of the smallpox epidemic, which killed untold thousands of

Aztecs, worked much to Cortés's advantage. He planned to return and lay siege to Tenochtitlan. And in the five months following his retreat from that city, his enemy grew weaker and weaker. Meanwhile, he methodically regrouped and expanded his own forces. Several hundred Spanish reinforcements arrived from Cuba. And large numbers of Tlaxcalans and other local natives joined the Europeans. Historian Ross Hassig explains how the two groups worked together, each contributing its own strengths:

Cortés's advantage lay less in his own men and arms, than in what they added to his Indian allies' men and arms. Aztec and Tlaxcalan armies were comparably armed, which often resulted in stalemates, and Cortés's men were too few to alter that balance. But unlike Indian arms, Spanish cannons, arquebuses, crossbows, and mounted lancers could all penetrate the opposing lines. So Cortés's primary contribution would be in punching through and disrupting opposing lines, while

The Role Played by Spanish Cannons

The Spanish cannons played an important role in the siege and capture of Tenochtitlan in 1521. Strictly from a tactical standpoint—that is, the number of people they killed—these big guns were not very useful in pitched battles with the Aztecs. However, the cannons did have a powerful psychological effect, mainly in situations in which groups of natives encountered these weapons for the first time. Put simply, the loud noises and smoke produced by the cannons at first frightened and/or disoriented the uninitiated. This is illustrated by what happened when Cortés demonstrated a cannon when he first arrived in Tenochtitlan:

[The explosion] caused great confusion in the city. The people scattered in every direction. They fled without rhyme or reason. They ran off as if they were being pursued. . . . They were all overcome by terror, as if their hearts had fainted. And when night fell, the panic spread through the city.

Over time, the natives got used to the cannons and were no longer awed by them. Still, these weapons did do substantial long-range damage to the city's temples, houses, and other buildings during the siege.

Quoted in Miguel Leon-Portilla, *The Broken Spears: The Aztec Account of the Conquest of Mexico*. Boston: Beacon, 1992, p. 66.

his Indian allies exploited breaches they could not create alone.[67]

Using this sort of military cooperation, the Spanish and Tlaxcalans proceeded to attack a number of local native city-states. Each, as a member of the imperiled empire, had recently been fortified with Aztec officers and soldiers. The onrushing Spanish and their Indian allies crushed each local army in its turn. And many of the leaders of the defeated cities swore allegiance to Spain, so that the number of Cortés's native supporters eventually swelled to as many as seventy thousand.

With this enormous army, the Spanish returned to Lake Texcoco late in 1520 and began getting ready to lay siege to the Aztec capital. Among these preparations was the launching of a fleet of small ships that had been assembled earlier and carted overland by the natives. These boats gave Cortés virtual control of the lake.

Broken Spears

The siege of Tenochtitlan began in earnest on June 1, 1521, and lasted eighty days. During the fighting, the city's residents, both men and women, fought courageously to preserve their homes and way of life. They were unable to withstand the tremendous onslaught launched by the enemy, however. One of Cortés's advantages was that his control of the lake allowed him to deny the besieged Aztecs the supplies of food and fresh water they

desperately needed. Another Spanish advantage was their cannons, which pounded away at the city's walls and buildings, reducing many of them to rubble. Finally, Cortés had at his disposal his numerous native allies, who kept him well supplied while, by their great numbers, helped to demoralize the city's defenders.

Finally, these odds proved too great for the beleaguered Aztecs. Their king, Cuitlahuac, had recently died of smallpox. So the unpleasant duty of surrender fell on his successor, Cuauhtémoc, a nephew of Montezuma. After his capture and submission, he was tortured by Cortés, who wanted to know the whereabouts of more gold; when the prisoner told his captors everything he knew about treasure, they killed him.

With the fall of the once-great city of Tenochtitlan, the Aztec realm simply ceased to exist. A handful of local towns briefly continued to resist, but faced with the prospect of attack by hordes of Cortés's native allies, they surrendered. As for the surviving Aztecs, most were in a state of shock or wracked by agonizing grief and sorrow. A forlorn Aztec poet captured their mood in this lament:

> Broken spears lie in the roads. We have torn our hair in grief. The houses are roofless now, and their walls are red with blood. . . . We have pounded our hands in despair against the adobe walls, for our inheritance, our city, is lost and dead. The shields of our warriors were its defense, but they could not save it.[68]

An artist's depiction of the eighty-day battle between the Spanish and the Aztecs for control of Tenochtitlan.

Only two years before, the Spanish had landed on Mexico's eastern shore. And many natives had harbored the hope that a beloved god-king of yesteryear had returned to usher the people into a golden age. Instead, in the words of one modern scholar, the "newcomers brought not the divine benevolence of Quetzalcoatl, but suffering, death, exotic disease, and slavery."[69]

The Aztecs in Later Centuries

At first, many Aztecs who had survived the capture of their towns and the collapse of their empire worried that their culture might be suppressed or even eradicated. Certainly the Spanish were quick to begin transforming central Mexico into a full-fledged colony, called Nueva España, or New Spain. Cortés made himself its governor. (In 1535 he was succeeded by the first of a series of colonial officials known as viceroys.) He made sure that all surviving Aztecs swore allegiance to the Spanish king, and Spanish became the official language of the colony. Also, a new Spanish capital, Mexico City, swiftly began to rise atop the rubble of the devastated Tenochtitlan. All of this was part of a large-scale, unstoppable process that transformed a major sector of the Americas into an extension of Spain itself. As Richard F. Townsend, a noted scholar of ancient Mesoamerica, puts it:

The conquest was a major turning point in American history, not simply because it marked the defeat of the Aztecs and the victory of the Spaniards, but because their violent encounter set in motion a new process which profoundly and permanently changed a whole cultural frame of existence. Mexico was the first and most systematically colonized of all the Spanish possessions in the New World. With surprising rapidity, new forms of economy, religion, and government were imposed on Mexico in the image and ideals of Spain.[70]

Yet despite the huge scope of this transformation, Aztec culture was far from eliminated. This was partly because it was so ingrained in the region and because the natives stubbornly clung to it in order to preserve their identity and minimize their despair. Because they continued to speak Nahuatl, they became known as the Nahua. And in many ways their culture combined with that of their conquerors. The blending of Aztec/Nahua and Spanish cultures, anthropologist Michael E. Smith explains, "was an active process in which people adopted some new traits and rejected others, just as they maintained some ancient practices and abandoned others."[71]

The New Social Ladder

One social environment in which the natives retained some of their old ways was in the *encomienda* system. The encomiendas were large agricultural estates set up by the early administrators of New Spain. Run by wealthy Spaniards called *encomenderos*, they used unpaid natives as menial laborers. The encomenderos were supposed to look after these workers and help to convert them to Christianity. But

A map of Tenochtitlan drawn by Cortés. After the Aztec defeat, the city was renamed Mexico City and was the capital of the Spanish colony New Spain.

Never Will It Be Forgotten

In 1609 a Nahua historian named Fernando Alvarado Tezozomoc, who was worried that the defeated Aztecs might be forgotten, wrote a poem, excerpted here, to commemorate them. He need not have worried because Aztec culture became a powerful component of modern Mexican culture.

> Thus in the future
> never will it [the memory of the Aztec] perish,
> never will it be forgotten,
> always we will treasure it, we, their children, their grandchildren,
> brothers, great-grandchildren, [and] descendants,
> we who carry their blood and their color,
> we will tell it, we will pass it on
> to those who do not yet live, who are yet to be born,
> the children of the Mexicans, the children of the Aztecs.

Fernando Alvarado Tezozomoc, *Cronica Mexicayotl*, trans. Adrian Leon. Mexico City: National University, 1975, pp. 4–5.

often they shirked this responsibility and instead abused and exploited the workers. Nevertheless, for the most part the landowners stayed out of the natives' personal lives. So the Nahuas continued to maintain many of their old political and social institutions, including the calpulli system in which they identified themselves with local neighborhoods.

Also, many of the Nahua steadily blended into colonial Spanish society, which inevitably had the effect of altering that society's makeup. At first, Mexican society was highly stratified, with a ladder of strictly separated social groups based on birth and parental ancestry. At the top was a small group of highly placed Spaniards who had been born in Spain and for the most part owned most of the land and wealth. Below them were the criollos, people who had been born in Mexico but whose parents and ancestry were Spanish. Comprising a sort of upper middle class, they were small landowners, merchants, and teachers.

The lower middle class was made up of mestizos, the products of mixed marriages between natives and Spaniards. (Initially, the mestizos were viewed as inferior to the criollos; but over time the mestizos grew in number until they made up the bulk of the population, and the barrier between the two groups began to blur.) Finally, at the bottom of the social ladder were the remaining full-blooded Indians, including the Nahuas.

Religious Conversion and Blending

Religion was another social area in which the cultures blended. The members of the upper classes, including the criollos, were Catholics from birth. But as part of state policy, many mestizos and all full-blooded Indians had to convert to Catholicism. This process was successfully accomplished over time. However, as California State University scholar Manuel Aguilar-Moreno points out, it proved to be a difficult task:

> The missionaries were confronted with many obstacles, [including] the fact that the religion they were hoping to replace was a complex, deeply rooted agricultural religion profoundly ingrained in the fabric of native life.[72]

As a result, the Nahuas and some mestizos held onto a number of their old beliefs and rituals. And religious practices in Mexico, like the social groups, came to combine elements from both the native and Spanish cultures. For example, the still-popular Mexican holiday called the Day of the Dead arose from a merger of the Catholic All Souls' Day

and the Aztec autumn festival, a remembrance of deceased ancestors.

Also, the natives came to associate the Aztec Earth goddess Coatlicue with the Christian Virgin Mary. That led to the emergence of the Virgin of Guadalupe, a sort of melding of the two female figures. "Today," says Aguilar-Moreno, "the Virgin of Guadalupe is considered to be the symbol of identity of the Mexican people, and she stands as the reigning patroness of the Americas."[73]

Birth of the Mestizo Nation

Over the centuries, meanwhile, Mexican society and culture increasingly came to be dominated by the mestizos. Yet the Nahua held onto many of their old ways while adapting, as needed, to the ones practiced by the mestizos. In this way, Smith says:

> The Nahua peoples have created their own dynamic, unique culture, and they continue to create it today, by meeting new challenges with the resources and knowledge available to them, of whatever origin. Some Nahuas have become completely integrated into the national culture, and others have kept to themselves in isolated villages. But in both Indian villages and Mexico City, much of the distinctive flavor of modern Mexican culture derives from the Aztec past.[74]

Many monuments to that proud past exist throughout modern Mexico. One of the more prominent examples is the old Aztec symbol of an eagle perched on a cactus that adorns the country's flag. Less conspicuous but no less moving is a small monument in Mexico City that rests on the traditional spot of the last Aztec resistance in Tenochtitlan. The inscription recalls that on August 13, 1521, while the last Aztec king, Cuauhtémoc, put up a heroic defense, the city fell to Hernán Cortés. "It was neither a triumph nor a defeat," the dedication reads. "It was the painful birth of the mestizo nation that is the Mexico of today."[75]

Notes

Introduction: A Clash of Similar Cultures

1. Bernal Diaz del Castillo, *The Conquest of New Spain*, trans. J.M. Cohen. New York: Penguin, 1963, p. 214.
2. Norman Bancroft-Hunt, *Gods and Myths of the Aztecs*. New York: Smithmark, 1996, p. 8.
3. Genesis 6:4.
4. Quoted in David Carrasco, *Daily Life of the Aztecs: People of the Sun and Earth*. Westport, CT: Greenwood, 1998, p. 40.
5. Manuel Aguilar-Moreno, *Handbook to Life in the Aztec World*. New York: Oxford University Press, 2006, p. xxi.

Chapter One: The Rise of the Aztecs

6. Diego Durán, *The History of the Indies of New Spain*, trans. Doris Heyden. Norman: University of Oklahoma Press, 1994, p. 20.
7. Aguilar-Moreno, *Handbook to Life in the Aztec World*, pp. 7, 10.
8. Michael E. Smith, *The Aztecs*. Cambridge, MA: Blackwell, 1996, p. 36.
9. Quoted in Durán, *History of the Indies of New Spain*, pp. 43–44.
10. Quoted in Eduardo M. Moctezuma, "Aztec History and Cosmovision," in *Moctezuma's Mexico: Visions of the Aztec World*, by David Carrasco and Eduardo M. Moctezuma. Niwot: University Press of Colorado, 1992, p. 19.
11. Brian M. Fagan, *Kingdoms of Gold, Kingdoms of Jade: The Americas Before Columbus*. New York: Thames and Hudson, 1991, p. 23.
12. Warwick Bray, *Everyday Life of the Aztecs*. London: B.T. Batsford, 1968, p. 116.
13. Fagan, *Kingdoms of Gold, Kingdoms of Jade*, p. 33.

Chapter Two: Society and Everyday Life

14. Carrasco, *Daily Life of the Aztecs*, p. 129.
15. Quoted in Moctezuma, "Aztec History and Cosmovision," pp. 24, 27.
16. Smith, *Aztecs*, p. 152.
17. Bernal Diaz del Castillo, *The Discovery and Conquest of Mexico, 1517–1521*, trans. A.P. Maudslay. New York: Farrar, Straus and Giroux, 1956, pp. 190–91.
18. Aguilar-Moreno, *Handbook to Life in the Aztec World*, pp. 355–56.
19. Quoted in Bernadino de Sahagun, *Florentine Codex: General History of the Things of New Spain*, vol. 8, trans. J.O. Anderson and Charles E. Dibble. Santa Fe, NM: School of American Research and University of Utah, 1950, p. 130.
20. *Codex Mendoza*, vol. 4, eds. Frances F. Berdan and Patricia R. Anawalt.

Berkeley: University of California Press, 1992, pp. 122–23, 124.

21. Hernán Cortés, *Letters from Mexico*, trans. Anthony Pagden. New Haven, CT: Yale University Press, 1986, p. 103.

Chapter Three: Myths and Religious Beliefs

22. Richard F. Townsend, *The Aztecs*. London: Thames and Hudson, 2000, p. 108.

23. Quoted in Miguel Leon-Portilla, *Aztec Thought and Culture*. Norman: University of Oklahoma Press, 1963, p. 44.

24. Some scholars have noted a number of marked similarities to aspects of the ancient Persian religion, Zoroastrianism. For details, see Don Nardo, *Greenhaven Encyclopedia of Ancient Mesopotamia*. Farmington Hills, MI: Greenhaven, 2007, pp. 257–59.

25. Quoted in David Carrasco, "The Sacrifice of Tezcatlipoca," in *To Change Place: Aztec Ceremonial Landscapes*, ed. David Carrasco. Niwot: University Press of Colorado, 1992, p. 42.

26. Carrasco, *Daily Life of the Aztecs*, p. 4.

27. Fagan, *Kingdoms of Gold, Kingdoms of Jade*, p. 32.

28. Smith, *Aztecs*, p. 221.

29. Diaz del Castillo, *Discovery and Conquest of Mexico*, p. 436.

30. Diego Durán, *Book of the Gods and Rites and the Aztec Calendar*, trans. Fernando Horcasites and Doris Heyden. Norman: University of Oklahoma Press, 1971, p. 122.

Chapter Four: Art, Literature, and Learning

31. James N. Corbridge, forward to *Moctezuma's Mexico*, by Carrasco

and Moctezuma, p. xi.

32. Moctezuma, "Aztec History and Cosmovision," p. 41.

33. Aguilar-Moreno, *Handbook to Life in the Aztec World*, p. 222.

34. Moctezuma, "Aztec History and Cosmovision," p. 66.

35. Quoted in Leon-Portilla, *Aztec Thought and Culture*, p. 73.

36. Quoted in Leon-Portilla, *Aztec Thought and Culture*, p. 142.

37. Durán, *History of the Indies of New Spain*, pp. 247–48.

Chapter Five: Weapons and Warfare

38. Aguilar-Moreno, *Handbook to Life in the Aztec World*, p. 98.

39. Durán, *Book of the Gods and Rites and the Aztec Calendar*, p. 197.

40. Durán, *History of the Indies of New Spain*, p. 554.

41. Quoted in Garcilaso de la Vega, *Florida of the Inca*, trans. John and Jeannette Varner. Houston: University of Texas Press, 1951, p. 597.

42. Enriquez de Guzman, *The Life and Acts of Don Alonzo Enriquez de Guzman, Knight of Seville*, trans. Clements R. Markham. London: Hakluyt Society, 1862, p. 99.

43. Quoted in Patricia de Fuentes, ed., *The Conquistadors: First-Person Accounts of the Conquest of Mexico*. Norman: University of Oklahoma Press, 1993, p. 169.

44. Quoted in Fuentes, *Conquistadors*, p. 169.

45. Quoted in Ross Hassig, *Aztec Warfare: Imperial Expansion and Political Control*. Norman: University of Oklahoma Press, 1988, p. 124.

46. Sahagun, *Florentine Codex*, p. 52.
47. Quoted in Hassig, *Aztec Warfare*, p. 124.

Chapter Six: The Arrival of the Spanish

48. Quoted in Miguel Leon-Portilla, ed., *The Broken Spears: The Aztec Account of the Conquest of Mexico*. Boston: Beacon, 1992, pp. 4–6.
49. Castillo, *Discovery and Conquest of Mexico*, p. 209.
50. *Codex Mendoza*, p. 34.
51. Quoted in Leon-Portilla, *Broken Spears*, pp. 16–17.
52. Quoted in Leon-Portilla, *Broken Spears*, p. 23.
53. Anonymous, "The First Letter," in Hernán Cortés, *Letters from Mexico*, trans. and ed. Anthony Pagden. New Haven, CT: Yale University Press, 1986, pp. 19–20.
54. Quoted in Leon-Portilla, *Broken Spears*, p. 30.
55. Quoted in Sahagun, *Florentine Codex: General History of the Things of New Spain*, vol. 12, trans. J.O. Anderson and Charles E. Dibble. Santa Fe, NM: School of American Research and University of Utah, 1950, p. 39.
56. Quoted in Fuentes, *Conquistadors*, p. 36.
57. Quoted in Leon-Portilla, *Broken Spears*, p. 51.
58. Quoted in Leon-Portilla, *Broken Spears*, p. 61.
59. Quoted in Fuentes, *Conquistadors*, p. 146.
60. Quoted in Leon-Portilla, *Broken Spears*, pp. 64–65.

Chapter Seven: Fall of the Aztec Empire

61. Quoted in Leon-Portilla, *Broken Spears*, pp. 68–69.
62. Quoted in Leon-Portilla, *Broken Spears*, pp. 74, 76.
63. Quoted in Leon-Portilla, *Broken Spears*, p. 79.
64. Hernando Cortés, "Second Letter of Hernando Cortés to Charles V," Early Americas Digital Archive, http://mith2.umd.edu/eada/html/display.php?docs=cortez_letter2.xml.
65. Quoted in Fuentes, *Conquistadors*, p. 154.
66. Quoted in Smith, *Aztecs*, p. 281.
67. Ross Hassig, "Tenochtitlan," in *The Seventy Great Battles in History*, ed. Jeremy Black. London: Thames and Hudson, 2005, p. 100.
68. Quoted in Leon-Portilla, *Broken Spears*, pp. 137–38.
69. Fagan, *Kingdoms of Gold, Kingdoms of Jade*, p. 37.

Epilogue: The Aztecs in Later Centuries

70. Townsend, *Aztecs*, pp. 7–8.
71. Smith, *Aztecs*, p. 296.
72. Aguilar-Moreno, *Handbook to Life in the Aztec World*, p. 388.
73. Aguilar-Moreno, *Handbook to Life in the Aztec World*, p. 389.
74. Smith, *Aztecs*, pp. 296–97.
75. Quoted in Carrasco, *Daily Life of the Aztecs*, p. 225.

Glossary

atlatl: A throwing stick used as a weapon by early native peoples around the world.

axis mundi: Translates as "world's navel." In Aztec mythology, it is the central region of the world.

Aztlan: The legendary homeland of the Aztecs before they began their journey into central Mexico.

calmecac: A school attended by the children of nobles.

calpullec: An elected official who administered a *calpulli*.

calpulli: A group of families making up a neighborhood. Also spelled *calpolli*.

chinampas: Fertile raised gardens created in swampy terrain.

cihuatlamacazqui: Female priests (or priestesses).

codex: A book.

conquistador: In late medieval times, one of a group of Spanish soldiers and adventurers.

criollos: In early New Spain, people born in Mexico but having Spanish parents and ancestry.

encomienda: A large agricultural estate in early New Spain.

glyph: A written sign that stands for a word, concept, or name.

harquebus: A primitive handheld gun used by the Spanish when they invaded the Aztec Empire. Also spelled arquebus.

ichcahuipilli: Cotton body armor.

macehualtin: Commoners in Aztec society.

mayeque: Poor, serflike laborers.

Mesoamerica: The modern term describing ancient central Mexico and neighboring regions.

mestizos: In early New Spain, people born of mixed marriages between natives and Spanish.

Mexica: The original name of the Nahuatl-speaking group later called the Aztecs.

mictlan: The underworld.

Nahua: In New Spain and modern Mexico, natives who are directly descended from the Aztecs and keep Aztec culture alive.

Nahuatl: The language spoken by the Aztecs and some related Mesoamerican peoples.

Nueva España: New Spain, the colony established in Mexico by the Spanish after defeating the Aztecs.

omen: A divine sign of an important impending event.

patolli: A popular board game utilizing beans as dice.

pipiltin: Members of the Aztec noble class.

pochteca: Traders or merchants.

quimichtin: Spies.

sacred precinct: A large central plaza containing temples and shrines.

telpochcalli: A school attended by the children of Aztec commoners.

tematlatl: A sling.

Tenochtitlan: The Aztecs' capital, situated on an island in Lake Texcoco.

Teotihuacan: Located east of Lake Texcoco, the largely abandoned Mesoamerican city that the Aztecs believed was a home of the gods.

teotl: A god.

tetecuhtin: A small group of elite Aztec nobles.

tianquiztli: A marketplace.

tlacotin: Aztec slaves.

tlacuilo: A scribe.

tlamacazqui: Male priests.

tlatoani: The Aztec king's title.

tlenamacac: Special priests who wielded the knife during human sacrifice.

ullamaliztli: A fast-moving, rough-and-tumble ballgame played in a large walled ball court.

ulli: The hard rubber ball used in the ball game *ullamaliztli*.

Valley of Mexico: A large, mountain-ringed basin in central Mexico.

yaochimalli: Aztec shields.

For Further Reading

Books

Manuel Aguilar-Moreno, *Handbook to Life in the Aztec World*. New York: Oxford University Press, 2006. A fact-filled look at Aztec culture and everyday life.

Norman Bancroft-Hunt, *Gods and Myths of the Aztecs*. New York: Smithmark, 1996. This well-researched volume explains Aztec deities, myths, and worship in clear terms.

David Carrasco, *Daily Life of the Aztecs: People of the Sun and Earth*. Westport, CT: Greenwood, 1998. A thoughtful, well-written account of life in the Aztec world.

Hernán Cortés, *Letters from Mexico*. Trans. and ed. Anthony Pagden. New Haven, CT: Yale University Press, 1986. A good modern translation of the letters in which Cortés describes his adventures to the Spanish king.

Brian Fagan, *The Aztecs*. New York: Freeman, 1997. Fagan, a noted scholar of archaeology, delivers a compelling overview of Aztec civilization.

Ross Hassig, *Mexico and the Spanish Conquest*. Norman: University of Oklahoma Press, 2006. Examines the military aspects of the Spanish conquest and the role played by native peoples.

Ross Hassig, *Time, History, and Belief in Aztec and Colonial Mexico*. Austin: University of Texas Press, 2001. A detailed study of Mesoamerican calendars, including the Aztec one, and how they affected the lives of the natives.

Miguel Leon-Portilla, ed., *The Broken Spears: The Aztec Account of the Conquest of Mexico*. Boston: Beacon, 1992. An excellent translation of several riveting surviving native accounts of the Spanish conquest. Highly recommended.

Charles C. Mann, *1491: New Revelations of the Americas Before Columbus*. New York: Vintage, 2006. Describes some of the latest discoveries about Aztec civilization.

John Pohl, *Aztec Warrior: A.D. 1325–1521*. Oxford, UK: Osprey, 2001. A beautifully illustrated presentation of Aztec weapons and military customs.

Michael E. Smith, *The Aztecs*. Cambridge, MA: Blackwell, 1996. An excellent overview of Aztec history and culture.

Hugh Thomas, *Conquest: Cortes, Montezuma, and the Fall of Old Mexico*. New York: Simon & Schuster, 1995. A thorough, well-researched treatment of the subject by one of its leading experts.

Richard F. Townsend, *The Aztecs*. London: Thames and Hudson, 2000. A superior, highly acclaimed study of this pivotal ancient people by a leading scholar.

Michael Wood, *Conquistadors*. Berkeley: University of California Press, 2000. A well-researched, fast-paced account of the conquistadors and their exploits, including the conquest of the Aztecs.

Internet Sources

Richard Hooker, "Civilizations in America: The Mexica/Aztecs," Washington State University, www.wsu.edu/~dee/CIVAMRCA/AZTECS.HTM.

Web Sites

Empires Past (http://library.thinkquest.org/16325). A good general reference on the empires of the past, including the ancient Aztecs with several links to articles about various aspects of their culture.

PBS (www.pbs.org/conquistadors). This Web site presents "Conquistadors, the Online Adventure," which includes a time line and a variety of activities for children in grades eight through twelve.

Index

Picture Credits

Cover, © Danny Lehman/Encyclopedia/Corbis
The Art Archive/Antochiw Collection of Mexico/Mireille Vautier, 87
The Art Archive/Dagli Orti, 40
The Art Archive/Museo Ciudad Mexico/Dagli Orti, 70, 89
The Art Archive/National Anthropological Museum Mexico/Dagli Orti, 55
The Art Archive/ National Archives Mexico/Mireille Vautier, 65
The Art Archive/Mireille Vautier, 34
The Art Archive/Palazzo Farnese Capraola/Dagi Orti, 7 (lower)
© Bettmann/Corbis, 6 (upper right and lower left), 29, 31, 73
© Stefano Bianchetti/Historical/Corbis, 75
The Gale Group, 9, 15
© Alfredo Dagli Orti/The Art Archive/The Picture Desk Limited/Corbis, 69
© Gianni Dagli Orti/Corbis, 10, 17, 19, 20, 53
© Gianni Dagli Orti/The Picture Desk Limited/Corbis, 39
© Werner Forman/Value Art/Corbis, 60
© The Gallery Collection/Corbis, 82-83
© Historical Picture Archive/Corbis, 52
© Wolfgang Kaehler/Corbis, 50
© Charles and Josette Lenars/Corbis, 49
© Philadelphia Museum of Art/Corbis, 35
© Kevin Schafer/Corbis, 16
© Stapelton Collection/Corbis, 26
© Stapelton Collection/Historical Picture Library/Corbis, 59
© Adam Woolfit/Corbis, 6 (lower right)
DEA Picture Library/DeAgostini Picture Library/Getty Images, 38
Dorling Kindersley/Getty Images, 63
The Library of Congress, 43, 76, 79

s acclaimed volumes on the ancient world, historian Don Nardo
nd edited many books for young adults about Native American his-
ulture, including *Early Native North Americans*, *The History of Weapons*
rfare: The Native Americans, *The Relocation of the North American Indian*, and
n American Indian Wars. Nardo also writes screenplays and teleplays and com-
ses music. He lives with his wife, Christine, in Massachusetts.